Scottish
Folk Tales

Scottish Folk Tales

Retold by
Ruth Ratcliff

FREDERICK MULLER LIMITED · LONDON

First published in Great Britain 1976 by
Frederick Muller Limited, London, NW2 6LE
Reprinted 1981

ISBN 0 584 62393 3

Printed in Great Britain by offset lithography
by Billing & Sons Limited
Guildford, London & Worcester

Contents

Glossary   6

Introduction   7

The Knight of the Glens and Bens and Passes   11

A Tale about the Son of the Knight of the Green Vesture   19

The Swarthy Smith of the Socks   40

Canobie Dick and Thomas of Ercildoun   49

Donald of the Burthens   53

The Son of the Strong Man of the Wood   57

Mac Iain Direach   73

The Importance of Fairy Names   84
    Habetrot
    Peerifool
    Whuppity Stoorie

The Wee Folk   97

Some strange Adventures with Mermaids, Dragons,
    Sprites, a Witch and a friendly Ghost   126

GLOSSARY

awa - *away*

bairn - *child*

bane - *bone*

bannock - *thick, round, flat cake (generally of oatmeal)*

ben - *hill, mountain*

bide - *wait, tarry*

blink - *moment (glimpse between showers)*

bluid - *blood*

bogle - *hobgoblin*

bonnie - *pretty*

brae - *hillside*

brose - *oatmeal mixed with boiling water - a kind of porridge*

brownie - *benevolent household sprite*

ca' - *call*

chalder - *a measure of grain*

coo (also: koo) - *cow*

cubby - *small enclosed place; a small basket*

cummer - *midwife*

dinna - *do not*

four-oories - *refreshment taken about four o'clock*

gart - *made*

gien - *given*

goodman (gudeman) - *head of the household; husband*

goodwife (gudewife) - *mistress of the house; wife*

a goo and a gitty - *baby-talk of endearment*

goud - *gold*

guid - *good*

ha' - *hall, house, home*

hae - *have*

hame - *home*

heather cowe - *tuft of heather*

hen-wife - *a woman in charge of poultry*

kail (kale) - *cabbage; also broth made of vegetables*

kemperman - *fighting man; king's bodyguard*

ken - *know*

knave-bairn - *male child*

knowe - *knoll*

laird - *landed proprietor*

lustiheid - *vigour*

mecht - *might*

meester - *master*

na - *not, no, none*

nae - *not, no, none*

naething - *nothing*

noo - *now*

owre - *over*

pawky - *shrewd, sly*

peerie - *very small*

pit - *put*

plaid - *a long piece of woolen cloth, worn over the shoulder, in tartan as part of Highland dress, small-checked, worn by Lowland shepherds*

pyke - *pick*

rivlin - *sandal of rough cow-hide*

shieling - *hut, cottage*

skirl - *frizzle*

sled - *low cart*

sleepit - *slept*

spunkie - *will-o'-the-whisp*

stane - *stone*

steading - *farmstead*

stot - *young bull*

strath - *valley or plain through which a river runs*

toom - *empty*

wad - *would*

wark - *work*

water-kelpie - *mischievous water-sprite; river-horse*

well-mowed - *well-stacked*

ye - *yourself, you*

yon - *that, those*

Introduction

Story-telling, it is said, is an art of the past. It flourished at a time when there was little other entertainment, and people gathered at nightfall in dimly lit rooms to listen to a story. Men, women and children were keen listeners, always asking for more.

In Scotland, as elsewhere, many tales were passed on orally for generations, until in the eighteenth and nineteenth centuries antiquaries realised that the tradition of telling stories was declining. These men then sought out people who kept the old stories fresh in their minds, and they wrote down what they heard. Eventually many tales appeared in printed collections. Sir Walter Scott, for example, was an enthusiastic collector of what in his time were called "antiquities", ballads, songs and tales. He gathered material from printed sources but also learnt much by word of mouth. He encouraged others to follow in his footsteps, and there is now a rich store of tales which have been told in Scotland for hundreds of years.

All tales in this volume have a particularly Scottish flavour, though similar tales do turn up in the traditions of other countries in slightly different form. What makes these stories special is their setting and their characters, and the characters' way of life.

Ghosts or witches inhabit crumbling grey houses or strong towers, some of them still standing in the border country. Bogles the Scottish goblins haunt deserted heaths and Will o' the Wisps flicker over marshes and moorlands. Fearful monsters and sea devils, often half beast, half man, dwell in the waters of streams and lochs, or shake their coats of shells, as they stride round stormy coasts. They delight in mischief, leading the weary traveller astray, even luring him to a watery grave, while mermaids and seal-maidens are not so much evil as capricious beings.

The Scottish fairies are a race of tiny exquisite creatures, clad in green. They live in woods and fields where they dwell in green fairy hills. There they hold their midnight feasts, dancing and making merry to the tinkling of pretty music. They may entice a mortal to take part in their revelleries, and some, thus beguiled, never return to their former homes. Others may leave Elfland only after seven years which to them may seem just a night.

The fairies are well loved though they can bring good or ill luck according to their fancy and to the way they have been treated by men. Those the fairies dislike will never prosper, and may even fall victim to one of their deadly arrows. The fairies may poison a farmer's beasts, blight his crops, and, worse still, spirit away a new-born babe, leaving a changeling in his place. Much cunning is needed to recover the human child.

The fairies lend or borrow household goods, and it is unlucky to refuse their request. It is risky to pass a fairy hill after sunset. Never must the fairies be called by their real name, and so they have become "the good neighbours" or "the wee folk" whose help can be relied upon by their friends.

The most helpful and, by and large, good-natured sprite of all is the brownie. A shaggy small being of wild and tousled appearance, he will attach himself to cottage, castle or farmhouse and live with the family, often for generations. During the day the brownie curls up in a quiet corner, but he works as a trusty servant in house or farm during the night when other folk are asleep. He will also silently watch the servants, guarding his master's interest, see to it that everything is done as it should be and that no dishonesty or carelessness is committed.

Every night a bowl of cream or some honey is set down for the brownie as a reward, but no conspicuous gifts must ever be offered to him. If given food, drink or clothing "as a hire" he instantly disappears, always with disastrous effects to the family he has left. He can be mischievous, and is ill-disposed towards the rites of the Christian church.

There are ways of getting rid of unwanted fairies: they vanish if their fairy hills are ploughed up, as they never tread ground ripped by plough-shares. They will not cross running water, and leaping over a stream may save one from an angry fairy host.

Tales from the Scottish Highlands, belonging to a larger Celtic tradition, have their own particular characteristics: Their language is highly poetic, retaining the rhythm of the Gaelic in which they were originally told.

Good storytellers everywhere repeat their tales word for word, and enjoy repeating certain turns of a story. Few storytellers surpass the man or woman who told their tales by the peat fire in a Highland *shieling*. Their tales are full of beautiful descriptive passages, so-called "ranns", relating conditions at sea, the fury of battle, or the quietness of evening descending on the countryside. These passages are repeated over and over again, and it is thought that they are remains of ancient Bardic poetry. Many of the heroes in these tales are over life-size, giants in fact, of super-human strength. A figure often met in Highland tales is the Hen-wife, the woman who looks after poultry on a farm or a big estate. She is frequently endowed with magic powers, part witch, part fairy, part "wise woman".

The stories of this volume are re-told from collections made during the ninetheenth century. A full list of sources follows, and a glossary for the Scottish words appears on page 6.

Sources

Campbell, J.F. Popular Tales of the West Highlands. 4 vols. Paisley and London 1890-93

Chambers, R. Popular Rhymes of Scotland. Edinburgh 1890

County Folk-Lore, Vol. VII. Fife, Clackmannan and Kinross-shires. (ed. J.E. Simpkins) London 1914

County Folk-Lore, Vol. III. Orkney and Shetland Islands. (ed. G.F. Black). London 1903

Cromek, R.H. Remains of Nithsdale and Galloway Song. London 1810

Douglas, Sir George, Scottish Fairy and Folk Tales. London n.d.

Gibbings, W.W. (publishers) Folk-lore and Legends, Scotland. London 1889

Henderson, G. The Popular Rhymes, Sayings and Proverbs of the County of Berwick. Newcastle-on-Tyne 1856

Henderson, W. Notes on the Folk-lore of the Northern Counties of England and the Borders. With an appendix on Household Tales by S. Baring-Gould. London 1856

Keightley, T. The Fairy Mythology. London 1850

Macdougall, J. (ed. G. Calder) Folk Tales and Fairy Lore. Edinburgh 1910

Macdougall, J. Folk and Hero Tales. Waifs and Strays of Celtic Tradition. Argyllshire Series No. III. London 1891

Scott, Sir Walter, Minstrelsy of the Scottish Border. 4 vols. Edinburgh and London 1932

The Knight of the Glens and Bens and Passes

There was once a rich knight whom the people called the Knight of the Glens and Bens and Passes. Opposite this knight's castle was a pretty green knoll, and when he was standing on the top of it, he could see every cow, horse and four-footed beast he possessed.

One fine sunny day he climbed the knoll and looked around, but not a living creature belonging to him was to be seen. He stood for a while where he was, wondering what had become of them, or where he could go in search of them. Then he cast a glance down the foot of the knoll, and what did he behold standing there but the White red-eared Hound.

"What is the cause of thy sadness today, Knight of the Glens and Bens, and Passes?" asked the White red-eared Hound.

"Great is that, and not little," replied the knight. "Every beast I had in the world is lost, and I know not where they have gone."

"If thou wilt give me one of thy daughters in marriage, I will bring every beast back to thee in an instant," said the White red-eared Hound.

The knight said he would if she herself were willing to have

11

him, and they went together to the castle. As soon as they entered the knight sent for his eldest daughter, and when she came, he spoke to her in gentle, coaxing words to see if she would marry the White red-eared Hound.

She marry the spotted dog? She would do nothing of the kind, not for the world. And without saying another word, she went out in great displeasure that so insulting an offer had been put before her.

After that the knight sent for the middle one. But as soon as she came in and heard his business, she turned on her heel, and sailed out without giving him as much as an answer. Then came the youngest, and when she heard the reason why she was sent for, she said to her father:

"I will marry him on condition he will bring your own property back to you."

Without delay people were invited to the wedding, and that same night the girl was married to the White red-eared Hound.

Early next day the knight went out to the top of the green knoll opposite the castle, and, on looking round, he beheld every beast that belonged to him, pasturing where he had last seen them. He returned in joy, and whom did he meet at the door but the very handsomest man he had ever seen. This was the White red-eared Hound of the night before, because the knight's young daughter had married him of her own free will. They went in together, and when the two other daughters of the knight saw the good-looking husband their sister had, they were sorry that they themselves had not married him.

The bridegroom and his wife stayed a few days longer with the knight, and then they went to his place, a fine large castle where they were as comfortable and happy as the day was long.

But, at the end of a day and a year, she made ready to go to her father's house, she was intending to remain there until her first baby was born. Before she left him, her husband told her not to tell anyone beneath the sun what his name was, for if she did, she would never see him again.

She promised that she would not and went on her way. Eventually she reached her father's house in safety, and not long after her baby was born.

Three nights after the event fairy music came about the house, by means of which the watchers were put asleep, and then there came in under the lintel a big hand which swept away the child, and left bread and a bottle of wine at the head of the bed.

When the time for her return home was at hand her sisters did all they could to see if she would tell them her husband's name. But she remembered her promise, and told them not. Then her husband himself came and took her away in his carriage.

At the end of another year and day she came again to her father's house to have another baby, and everything happened to her as on the first occasion.

Then she came the third time to her father's house. And before she left home her husband again gave her strict orders not to tell his name to a living being. She promised that she would not, but her sisters threatening to burn her if she hid it from them any longer, put her in such a fright that she at last confessed that Summer-under-Dew was what he was called.

On the third night after the child was born, fairy music again came about the house, and while the watchers were asleep, the hand took away the child. But this time if left neither bread nor wine, and the husband came not, as he was wont, to take his wife home. By this she knew that she had done wrong in giving her husband's name to her sisters.

As soon as she could move, she set out towards home, but when she reached it, she found no living creature about the castle. She knew that all was not well, and without

13

further delay, she went in search of her husband. She travelled onwards all day long, until there was blackening on the soles of her feet and holing in her shoes; the little nestling, rolled-up, yellow-topped birds were taking to rest at the foot of the bushes, and the tops of the trees, and the pretty nimble squirrels were choosing as best they could a place for themselves, though she, the daughter of the Knight of the Glens and Bens and Passes, was not.

Then she cast a glance before her, and saw far from her a little house with a light, but if it was far from her, she took not long to reach it.

The door was open, and a good fire in the middle of the floor. She went in, and the mistress of the house, sitting beyond the fire, said:

"Come up, poor woman, thou art welcome to stay here tonight. Thy husband was here last night, he and his three children. There is an apple which he left with me for thee."

The kind woman treated the stranger well. She put warm water on her feet, and a soft bed under her side, and in the morning, when she set her on the head of the way and was bidding her good-bye, she handed her scissors and said:

"There are scissors for thee, and when thou wilt make the first cut with them, thou shalt let them go, and after that they will of themselves cut the cloth in the shape thou wishest to give it."

Then the girl turned away and travelled onwards all day long till there was blackening on the soles of her feet and holing in her shoes; the little nestling, rolled-up, yellow-topped birds were taking to rest at the foot of the bushes and in the tops of the trees, and the pretty nimble squirrels were choosing as best they could a place for themselves, though she, the daughter of the Knight of the Glens and Bens and Passes, was not. In the dusk she gave a glance before her, and saw far from her a little house with a light, but if it was far from her, she took not long to reach it.

The door was open, and a good fire on the middle of the floor. She went in, and the mistress of the house, who was sitting beyond the fire, said:

"Come up, poor woman, thou art welcome here tonight. Thy husband was here last night, himself and his three children."

She got well cared for by the mistress of the house. She put warm water on her feet, and a soft bed under her side, and when she was leaving in the morning she was handed a thimble, and the woman said:

"There is a thimble for thee, and as soon as thou hast made one stitch with it, thou shalt let it go, and it will work afterwards alone."

Then the girl turned away and kept on her journey at a good pace until she saw sometime during the day her husband and their children before her.

Then she hardened her pace, and stretched away after him with all her might. He looked behind him, and when he saw her coming, he and those with him hastened their steps, but though they did, she was gradually gaining upon them. He knew not how he would take himself off from her until he beheld a smithy, and, in passing, told the smiths to put an impediment on the woman who was coming after him. They replied that they would do that, and when she reached them, they seized her and put so tight a hoop about her middle that it was with difficulty she could even take a step.

However, as soon as she got out of their hands, she went away again as well as she could until she came to a steep climb in her path. Getting up the brae with a struggle, the hoop burst, and then she said:

"Though my girdle has burst, my heart has not."

She then went off with a rush, and kept travelling until there was blackening on the soles of her feet and holing in her shoes; the little nestling rolled-up, yellow topped birds were taking to rest at the foot of the bushes and in

16

the tops of the trees, and the pretty nimble squirrels were choosing the best place they could for themselves, though she, the daughter of the Knight of the Glens and Bens and Passes, was not. At last she saw far away from her a little house with a light in it, but if it was far from her, she took not long to reach it.

She went in, and the mistress of the house said to her:

"Oh, hast thou come, daughter of the knight? Thou art welcome here tonight. Thy husband was here last night, himself and his children, and they went away early in the morning."

She was well treated by the mistress of the house, who put warm water on her feet, and a soft bed under her side, and when she was leaving in the morning, the woman said:

"There is a needle for you, and after thou hast made one stitch with it, thou shalt let it go, and it will then sew alone."

Then the girl went once more on her journey, and kept going forward till she came to what appeared to be a gentleman's place. She saw a little house before her, and made straight for it. What was it but the house of the gentleman's hen-wife. She went in, and got leave to stay.

She was not long there before she noticed that there was a great stir among the people round about. She enquired of the hen-wife what was the cause of the stir, and the hen-wife told her that the man who owned the place was coming home to be married that very night.

The girl thought for a moment, but whatever she suspected she kept her opinion to herself. She got out the scissors, the thimble, and the needle, and set them going. In a short time there was not a person about the place who did not come to see the curious things the woman in the hen-wife's house had brought with her.

Among the rest came the newly-married couple, and when the bride saw the sewing implements going of their own accord, nothing would please her but to get them for herself.

17

By now the girl knew that her suspicion was right, and that the bridegroom was her own dear husband. And so she thought of a trick to keep the two apart, to be able to ask forgiveness from the man she loved.

She would get the things, she told the bride, but on one condition only, namely that she would suffer her — the strange woman — to sit up for three nights in succession in the bridegroom's own room.

This was agreed upon, but the bride took care to give the bridegroom a drink that would put him in so sound a sleep that he would not hear a syllable of anything the strange woman might say.

However, on the third night, the eldest boy having found out that the strange woman was his mother, spilt the sleeping draught and filled the cup with clear water. Then his father remained wide awake, so that he heard the strange woman saying:

"Summer-under-Dew, dost thou not pity me? I, that has travelled the world after thee."

At once he recognised his own dear wife, and he forgave her disobedience.

A great merry feast was prepared for the next day, and the new bride was allowed to keep the scissors, thimble and needle, and was married to Summer-under-Dew's brother.

It was a grand wedding, and when it was over they sent me home with little paper shoes on a causeway of glass. That wasn't merry at all!

A Tale about the Son of the Knight of the Green Vesture

His heroic deeds which were famed on earth seven years before he was born.

A long time ago there lived a gentleman who had a fine place and an abundance of cattle and poultry. In his time, landlords like him valued poultry so highly that they were in the habit of keeping about them a shrewd woman whom people called the Hen-wife. This gentleman also had a Hen-wife who was very shrewd, and who had a pretty young boy whom she called her son, and who called her his mother.

The boy was growing up a fine lad, and gave promise of becoming a brave man. But far and near he got no other name than Son of the Hen-wife; yet that gave him not the least annoyance.

The Hen-wife was well off under the landlord, having a house, three cows, and everything else she needed. When the boy grew up a young lad he was accustomed to go away with the cows and herd them all day. On a certain day he drove them further away than he was wont to do, to a place where the pasture was exceedingly good. As soon as the cattle took to the grass, he climbed a pretty knoll where he would be in sight of them and sat down. He passed a great part of the day

19

there, taking delight in everything he saw. At last he beheld, ascending from the hollow under him to the place where he was sitting, a young maiden with the red of the rose on her cheek and golden hair hanging down in ringlets over her shoulders.

She reached the place where he was sitting, and after bidding him good day, said that he must be lonely herding the three cows. He answered her readily, saying that he was not lonely now since she had come to be with him.

She then asked him whether he would sell her one of the cows. But he told her that he could not do that as his mother would scold him.

"Oh no, if thou get her value for the cow."

"And what wilt thou give me for her?"

"I will give thee a stone of virtues, a magic stone."

"What are the virtues that the stone possesses?"

"There is not a virtue that thou needest which thou shalt not find as long as thou keep it, and there is not a place where thou biddest thyself and as many as thou likest in which thou shalt not be in an instant."

"Let me have a look at the stone."

The maiden handed him the stone, and it was beautiful to look at. The boy took hold of it, and thought that he would test it before he gave the cow for it. He was thirsty at the time, and thought that he would like a drink from the spring of the Red-stone behind his mother's house. No sooner had the thought come into his mind than he was sitting beside the well. He took a drink, and returned in the same way in which he came. He then gave the cow for the stone and was perfectly well satisfied with the exchange which he had made.

Then the maiden of the rose-red cheeks went away with the cow that she bought, and he returned home with the other two cows in the dusk. When his mother saw that he had only two, she asked him about the third, and he told her that he had sold the cow.

"What did you get for it?" asked his mother.

"A stone," he answered.

When his mother saw the stone and could not understand its use, she flew into a rage and scolded the boy dreadfully. He listened calmly to every word she said and spoke not a syllable against her. When her wrath had abated, she told the boy to put in the two cows so that they should be milked. He did so, and that night the two cows gave as much milk as the three had done before.

In the morning, after he had taken his breakfast, his mother told him to drive the cows back to the place where they had been the day before. He went away with them, and left them in the very same spot. As soon as they arrived the cattle took to the pasture, and he sat down on the same knoll on which he was on the past day.

About the time when he first saw the maiden he saw her this day again ascending the hollow beneath him. She reached the place where he was sitting and asked him whether he would sell another of his cows.

"I will not," said he, "because my mother gave me a frightful scolding on account of the one I sold yesterday."

"Oh, if thou get her value for her, she will not scold thee."

"What then wilt thou give me for her?"

"I will give thee a healing jewel for her."

"What sores will the jewel heal?"

"Any sores on thy flesh or on thy skin, any disease of the body or of the mind it will heal when thou dost rub it against thee."

There was a wound on the lad's toe, and he asked the maiden to show him the jewel. He got it, and as soon as he rubbed it against his toe it was healed. Then he gave her the cow and was perfectly pleased with the exchange he had made.

When evening came, he went home with the remaining

21

cow. His mother met him on the way back and asked him what he got for the cow he had sold. He said that he got a jewel for her.

When she heard this, if she flew into a rage the day before, she flew into a sevenfold worse rage this day. She calmed down at last and told the boy to put in the remaining cow so that she might be milked. He did that, and the one cow gave as much milk as the three had done before.

The morning after the mother told the lad to drive the one cow to the place in which he had been the previous day. He went away, and again sat down on the knoll as he was wont to do. Again the maiden came and asked whether he would sell the only cow he had left.

"Oh, I dare not, for I got a terrible scolding on account of the last one I sold."

"Oh, thou shalt not get a scolding if thou get value for the cow."

"And what then wilt thou give me for her?"

"I will give thee a little bird-net."

"What sort of birds will the net catch, or how is it to be set?"

"Thou hast nothing to do but to spread it on the tops of the bushes and leave it there all night; and in the morning it will be full of all kinds of birds thou hast ever seen or heard, and there shall be in it twelve birds the like of which thou hast never seen or heard."

So the boy gave the cow for the net.

When his mother saw that he came home without any cow at all with him, she could not utter a word, but she cast a woeful look at him. He was very sorry that he displeased her so much, but he was sure that she would be satisfied when she saw the number of birds he would have in the net the next morning.

As soon as he got up he went to see the net, which he had set on the night before, and such a sight of birds he never saw till that moment. He went home with them, and when his mother saw what a number he had, she asked of him where he found them.

"I caught them in the net," he answered.

"And wilt thou get more with it?"

"I will get this number every time that I set it."

Now his mother was better pleased, and they had never been so well off with the milk of the cows as they were with the flesh of the birds.

The lad grew up a comely man in appearance, and wise in his conduct. The gentleman who employed his mother as Hen-wife took a liking to him, and he made him a footman in his house. He did well in his new situation, and everybody about the house respected him.

Now the gentleman had a daughter whom people called Berry-eye. She was exceedingly beautiful, and the lad fell deeply in love with her. She also fell in love with him, but she would never acknowledge that she had done so, because he was only the Hen-wife's son. She would go out of his way and hide herself in every bush lest he should see her. But he carried the magic stone, and with its help he would be found standing at her side wherever she happened to be. But she would then call for her father, and the lad had to go away lest he should be seen. This often happened, but on a certain day he wished that he should be with her in the house, and in an instant he was there. As soon as she saw him, she tried to call for her father, but before she had time to utter a word, he took her in his arms, and said:

"Would that thou and I were in the Green Isle at the Extremity of the Uttermost World, where thy father would not hear thy voice, and my mother would not say that I was her son."

Without knowing how, they were in the twinkling of an eye in the Green Isle at the far end of the world.

They were there for a good while living on the fruit of

23

the trees. But on a certain day, while they were sitting together on a hillside and looking at the ocean before them, he laid down his head on her lap and slept.

While he was sleeping the girl began to wonder how they could have come to the place, and in the end she supposed that he must have had magic or something possessing wonderful properties by which he had drawn them to where they were now. As soon as this occurred to her, she searched his clothes to see if she could find anything in them to confirm her suspicion. She opened his clothes, and found the stone and the jewel carefully hidden on his chest. She looked at them — and they were beautiful to behold — and she thought that it must have been those things that carried them to the isle. She then took her scissors, and cut away the front of her dress with them, and left the piece under his head. As soon as she got up, she said:

"Would that I were once more at my father's house," and before the words went out of her mouth she was in her father's house.

When the lad woke up he looked round to see if he could behold her, but he looked in vain as nowhere could he see the girl. He then looked on the ground and saw the front of her dress where she had left it under his head. He quickly put his hand on his breast and found it open and the stones taken away. He now knew how the matter stood, and feeling sorrowful and downcast, he wished that he had never come to the place, for he had neither means nor plan of getting out of it.

On a certain day he was wandering beside the shore, when he noticed a clump of trees near a wood which was before him. He reached the clump and saw in it trees bearing fruit such as he had not seen since he came to the island. On some of the trees were the most beautiful apples he had ever seen, and on others were the ugliest. He was downcast and sick with grief and weariness, and he thought that he would eat one of the beautiful apples to see if he would be the better of it. But as soon as he ate it, his feet began to shake, and his flesh to melt off his bones. He thought that as death was inevitably before him, and as he was in great pain, he would eat one of the ugly apples to see if it would hasten the approach of death. But as soon as he ate the ugly apple his flesh ceased to melt away, and his bones to shake, and before he had eaten another of them, he was as whole and sound as he ever was. He now saw that if he lost a jewel, he had found a cure for all ill. He at once began to make creels, and when they were ready, he filled them with the apples. Then he put them in a safe place, in the hope that they might yet be of use to him.

On a certain day he saw far out on the ocean a ship making straight for the island. He put up signals to see if he could draw the attention of the crew towards him, and when she came within hearing distance, he began to shout to the sailors. They noticed him, and sent a boat ashore where he was. The boat's crew asked him what sent him there, or how did he come thither.

"The vessel I sailed in was lost, and I alone got ashore on the island," answered the lad.

The sailors asked what was he doing on the vessel.

"I was a physician," said he.

At that the crew was very pleased, saying that their captain was sick, and had been given up by their own physician.

"Perhaps thou canst do something for him."

"We shall see what can be done when we reach him," replied the lad.

He put the creels in the boat, and when he reached the ship, he left them in a safe place on board her. He then took one or two of the apples with him in his pocket and went into the captain's room. He looked at him and said that if the captain would take what he gave him, he would be cured.

The captain answered that he would take anything that would do him good. Then the physician gave him a bite of one of the beautiful apples, and as soon as he ate it his flesh and skin began to melt away off him. When the crew saw this, they were going to tie the physician to the mast, and scourge him to death with the end of a rope. But he begged them to give him another hour, and said that if he did not heal the captain in that time, they might then bind him and scourge him to death if they pleased. They told him that he should get the time he asked for, and even till night.

Then they went away and left him alone.

He shut the door on them, and began to cure the captain with the ugly apples, and ere the end of the hour was come, he had him as strong and healthy as he was before he grew ill. When the crew saw this, they were very obedient to the physician, and knew not what they could do to please him. The captain asked what did the lad wish them to do for him. He answered that he wanted nothing but that they should land him in the haven from which he had come. They at once put the ship about, and made straight for the haven he named.

When they reached it, he took the baskets and went ashore. Taking farewell from the captain and his men, he made straight for the place whence he had departed.

He set up as a physician, and began to heal sick people. None of his old acquaintances knew him, but his name went far and near as a good physician who was healing people of every sickness and all sores which afflicted them.

On a certain day word came to him from the gentleman he had once served; he was to come in haste to visit his daughter who was at that time very ill. He went away without delay and soon reached the gentleman's house. He entered the room where the daughter was, and having examined her, said that she was suffering under a strange malady.

"Thou hast committed theft," said he to her, "and until thou confess it, thou canst not be healed."

She answered that she was not aware of having ever committed theft. To which the physician replied that she must have taken something from somebody that was very valuable to him. Then the girl remembered the stones which she took from the Hen-wife's son in the Green Isle, and she told the physician everything that happened between them. He asked where the stones were which she took from his breast.

"There, on the window-ledge," she answered.

Instantly the physician got the stones and put them in his pocket, saying:

"Since thou hast told the truth, thou canst be healed."

Then he gave her some of the ugly apples, and before the next night came, she was well and healthy.

The physician pleased the girl's father so well that nothing in existence would satisfy him but that the physician would marry Berry-eye, his daughter. The physician agreed to take her, and the marriage day was fixed.

The lad did not reveal himself to his mother until that very night when he went to her house, and told her that he was going to marry Berry-eye, with the full consent of her father.

"But, mother," said he, "do not let on that I am your son until the marriage is over."

She promised him that and rejoiced at his arrival.

The wedding day came at length, and among those preparing the feast none was busier than the Hen-wife. During the day Berry-eye came in, accompanied by her father and the physician, and when she noticed that the old woman was first in everything, she went over to where she was and said sharply to her:

"Woman, I know not what business you have here. You had better go out for the present."

The Hen-wife turned on her and replied fiercely:

"What dost thou say? I know not where I should have business unless I have it here preparing for my son's wedding."

Berry-eye gave a painful shriek, she sprang to her father and laid hold of his hand. When she recovered her breath, she said to the Hen-wife:

"Is he your son, woman?"

"Yes," said the Hen-wife.

"Well, if he is, I will not marry him."

Sadness now fell on all present and especially on the lad. But ere another got an opportunity to speak, the Hen-wife said:

"He is not my son, but the Son of the Knight of the Green Vesture, performing heroic deeds which were famed on earth seven years before he was born, and who fell fighting in the play of swords against the Fierce Earl of the Wood-of-Masts, by a stroke in the back from the Eldest Son of the Fierce Earl, and I was nurse with him at that time, and when he was slain, I fled with this lad, and I nursed him and brought him up, and now he is able to avenge his father's death, and to select his chosen sweetheart for wife."

When the lad heard what the Hen-wife said, he took courage and said to her:

"Woman, if I am that, I will not marry her."

"May all women be cursed for their chatter," said the gentleman.

The Son of the Knight of the Green Vesture now had his jewel and the magic stone in his bosom, and he gave his word and oath that he would neither return nor stop for the sake of man or thing until he saw a fairer maiden than Berry-eye. Then he departed.

He kept going forward, ascending bens and hills and hillocks, and going through holes and glens and hollows, until he reached an exceedingly fine place. He did not go to the castle that was there, because he knew not what or who might be before him. But the night was coming, and therefore he went for shelter among the bushes which were behind the castle. As soon as he reached them, he saw the fairest maiden he ever beheld coming towards him. Her eyes were like the heath-berry, and her bosom whiter than the snow of one night. She passed without noticing him, but he got a sight of her which drove Berry-eye completely out of his memory.

After she had gone out of sight, he left the bushes and went away to see if he could meet anyone who would tell him who she was. He did not go far before he beheld a very beautiful damsel having a gold comb in the back of her head, driving cows into a byre. He approached her, and inquired about the maiden whom he had seen walking though the bushes behind the castle.

She answered that she was Smooth-brow, daughter of the King of the Green Mound, and that she had been very anxious for the last six weeks.

"What is the cause of her anxiety?" asked the young man.

"Come into the byre, and I will tell thee that."

He went in, and she gave him a drink of milk. Then she said that the cause of Smooth-brow's anxiety was a dream which she had had almost a year before.

"She dreamt that she was walking through the bushes behind the castle, when she beheld a brave hero coming towards her, his countenance as the sun, and his appearance like that of a lion. His curly hair was as black as a raven's, and whiter than milk was his bosom."

She then told the young man that there were many seeking Smooth-brow's hand in marriage, and that her father wished her to marry a certain one of them. But she had vowed that she would never marry until she beheld the countenance of the hero she saw in her sleep. This did not please her father, and he gave her a day and a year to select her choice of a sweetheart, and said to her that if she let that time pass without making any choice for herself, she must thereafter take his choice.

The time had now run out except four days from tomorrow, and this was causing the maiden such great anxiety that she was taking a walk through the bushes every evening to see if she could meet the brave knight who appeared in her dream. That very morning she had almost yielded to her father, but of the last minute she had decided to go to a Wise Woman first. She told the Wise Woman her dream and everything else from beginning to end, whereupon the Wise Woman said:

"Do not lose courage, but run thy race to its end, for the brave hero's time has not yet come."

Then the young man said to the damsel:

"Where can I get an opportunity of speaking to her?"

"Tomorrow night watch well the place in which thou sawest me tonight."

He stayed that night in a place which the damsel provided for him, and next day kept out of everybody's way until evening, the time when he first saw the maiden.

He then went to the back of the castle, and waited there but a short time when he saw Smooth-brow coming. As soon as he caught sight of her, he went towards her, and stretched out his arms to embrace her.

She looked in his face, and as if she had always known him, said:

"Hast thou come at last?"

She put her arms about his neck, and nestled her head in his bosom. Then she told him about all her misery, and asked him to go with her, so that she would find him a place in which he might stay the night.

He went with her, and she put him in a secret chamber where he was to stay until her time had run out.

Next morning she was more cheerful than she was wont to be.

This the Wise Woman noticed. She asked her whether she had been among the bushes the night before.

The girl replied that she was, and that she had found the brave hero of her dream.

"Run thy race to its end, that he may take thee with victory," said the Wise Woman.

Then the maiden went to the room where the young hero was, and while they were talking, there was a loud noise, as if of an army approaching.

The young man wondered what it was all about, and the girl explained that there had come word of enemies marching against the castle. However, the Red-haired, Squint-eyed Cook had taken it in hand to turn the enemy back, and he was making ready to go.

"What does the enemy seek," asked the young man.

"They are from the Big Son of the Fierce Earl of the Wood of Masts, and if my father has no man to repel them, I and half the kingdom are his."

When the young hero heard the name of the Eldest Son of the Fierce Earl mentioned, he trembled on his feet, his eyes kindled in his head, he clenched his fists, and said that he must go and see how carrying arms became the cook.

"Thou shalt stay here, and show not thyself to thy father until I return." And having said that, the young man went out and took a back road to meet the cook.

The cook had not gone far from the castle when the young man overtook him. He asked where he was going.

The cook answered with great vigour that it was he who was driving back the enemy who was coming to the King of the Green Mound from the Eldest Son of the Fierce Earl of the Wood of Masts, and that when he had driven back the enemy, Smooth-brow and half the kingdom would be his.

"Right enough," said the young man; "but wilt thou lend me thine arms to see how they suit me?"

"I will indeed," replied the cook, and handed his arms to the young man.

And it was seen that the young hero was the one who had the true right to them.

"How didst thou know that I was going away?" asked the cook.

"I heard the noise which the point of thy sword made against one of the pots when thou wast going out."

"Oh, how pleased I am!" said the cook.

When they were nearing the place where the two parties would meet, they saw their opponents approaching. Then the young man said to the cook:

"Thou hadst better put these arms on before they come nearer."

The cook gave a look, and when he saw the Eldest Son of the Fierce Earl and his men approaching, he said:

"No, no. Leave them on thee, for they become thee better. Hide me in some place or other."

There was a precipice near them, and a large cleft in the face of the rock, so the young man thrust the cook into the cleft and said:

"Stay thou there until I return."

Then the Son of the Knight of the Green Vesture advanced to meet the Eldest Son of the Fierce Earl. They attacked each other, but with the third stroke of his sword the Son of the Knight of the Green Vesture swept the head off the Eldest Son of the Fierce Earl. He then assailed the men, and having killed them all, he lifted the head of the Earl's Son on the point of his sword, and returned carrying it over his shoulder.

He reached the cook and told him to come out of the cleft. The cook came as he was bidden. He looked first at the young man and then at the head and said:

"Thou hast a head!"

"Yes," replied the young hero.

"His eyes are open! Will he meddle with me?"

"I do not think he will at present."

Then they went away together, and when they came near the castle, the brave hero said to the cook:

"Thou hadst better put on these arms now, and take the head in to the king." The cook put on the arms, and the hero handed him the head in the parting.

"We are not going to part in that manner," said the cook. "Thou shalt go with me to the cooking-place, that you mayst get something I will give thee. When I am the king, thou shalt be my cook."

The young man went in with him, and when they entered the cooking-place the cook gave him a large bunch of white tow, and said:

"Thou shalt keep this to wipe the perspiration off thy face. When I was a cook, the man who gave me a bunch of tow I esteemed a friend."

"I also esteem him a friend," said the hero, and they parted.

The cook took his way with the head to the king, and the Son of the Knight of the Green Vesture went to Smooth-brow. He found her where he had left her, but told her nothing further than that the cook had driven back the enemy.

When the king saw the cook having the head with him, he was very well pleased, and said that he would be as good as his promise to him. But the cook was in a great hurry to have the marriage completed without delay. The king told him to have patience until they had dined, and said that he would then do everything as he had promised. The table was laid, and they all sat down to dinner. But before it was past, word came from the Second Son of the Fierce Earl, challenging the king's men, and saying that if he was victorious, he would have Smooth-brow and half of the kingdom.

The king now sent for his men, and asked who would go and drive back the enemy. The cook cried out:

34

"Who, if not I? I drove back the enemy once, and I will do it again."

"Right enough," said the king. "Do that, and I will be as good as my promise to thee."

Next morning the cook made ready to depart, and when he was under full armour, he gave a great stroke to the pot and went away. The young man heard the sound, and said to Smooth-brow that he must go and see what was the matter.

"Thou need'st not," said she; "it is only the cook going to repel another band of men today."

"I will go and see how the arms become him, but do thou not show thy face to thy father until I return." Then he went out after the cook.

This day he suffered him to advance a good distance before he overtook him. The cook's step was getting slower, and his look was oftener behind him the longer the young man was in coming. At length he saw him from afar, and stood until he overtook him.

"Didst thou hear the stroke I gave the pot today?" asked the cook.

"Yes, it was that which took me away," replied the young man.

When they were approaching the trysting-place the cook said:

"Thou wouldst do well to put on these arms, for they become thee better." Then the young man put on the arms, and when they saw the men coming, the cook cried:

"There they are! There they are! Hide me."

There was a soft marsh a short distance off, and when they reached it, the young man thrust the cook feet foremost in the ground beneath a dripping bank overgrown with heather, and told him to stay there until he should return.

Then the hero met the Second Son of the Fierce Earl, and with the second stroke of his sword threw his head off from his shoulders. He next attacked the men, and he did not stop until he left not a man of them alive. He then seized the head of the Fierce Earl's Second Son by the hair, and carried it with him on his shoulder. He reached the cook and called on him to come out from under the bank.

The cook came, and said:

"Thou hast a head again today. Oh, it grins! Will it meddle with me?"

"It will not at present," said the young hero, and they returned the way they came. When they were near the castle, the brave hero told the cook to put on the arms, and take the head to the king. He put on the arms, and when the hero was going to part with him, he said:

"We are not going to part in that manner. Thou shalt go with me to the cooking-place, that thou mayst get something that I will give thee."

When they entered the cook gave him a dumpy spoon, and said:

"Keep that until thou art cook with me. When I was a cook, I regarded the man who gave me a dumpy spoon as a friend."

"I also regard him as a friend," said the hero, and they parted.

The cook took his way in where the king was, and the Son of the Knight of the Green Vesture went to Smooth-brow.

The king rejoiced greatly when he saw that the cook had been victorious a second time. He said that he would be as good as his promise to him. But nothing would satisfy the cook but that the marriage be arranged without any further delay.

The king said to him:

"Thou art tired after the hard fight thou hast fought, and we are hungry. We shall take dinner first, and after that I will be as good as my promise to thee."

But before the dinner was over, word came from the

36

Young Son of the Fierce Earl, challenging the king's men and saying that if he was victorious Smooth-brow and half the kingdom would be his.

The king was now seized with great alarm, and he sent once more for his men. He told them that a challenge had come from the Young Son of the Fierce Earl, and said that he would be as good as his promise to the man who would drive the enemy back.

The cook sprang up, and facing the king, he said:

"Who should drive back the enemy, if not I? I turned the enemy back twice already, and I will do it again."

"Very right," said the king; "I will do as I promised."

When the cook got his armour and his arms on, if he gave a stroke to the pots on the two preceding days, he gave them a seven times louder stroke this day. He then turned away but the young man was in no hurry to follow him. He went off at last, but though he did go, he hid himself until they were nearing the place of the meeting. There he saw the cook sitting down.

He went up to him with a lively step.

"Hast thou come at last?" asked the cook.

"Yes," said the hero.

"It is I who was afraid that thou wouldst not come at all. Put on these arms, for verily they become thee better."

"I daresay they will today," replied the hero.

The arms were scarcely on him when they beheld the enemy approaching, and a very fierce-looking man was at their head.

"Oh, hide me!" shouted the cook. "Put me out of their sight."

Near them was a stagnant pond, and he thrust the cook down to the neck in the pond, and said:

"If thou art any way hard pressed, take thy head under water, but if not, stay as thou art."

The parties then met, and with one stroke of his sword

the Son of the Knight of the Green Vesture threw the sword out of the hand of the Fierce Earl's Young Son. He then took hold of him, and tied him up. He left him bound and turned to face the men. He made a fierce attack on them and left not a man alive to tell the tale of woe. Then he lifted the Earl's Son on his shoulder and reached the cook with him.

The cook came ashore, wet and dirty and covered with the white moss of the marsh, and joined the hero on the way back. As soon as they came in sight of the castle the hero said:

"Thou hadst better put on the arms now, and take this man in to the king."

When the cook put the arms on, he looked at the man, and when he saw him moving, he cried:

"Oh, he is alive! He will meddle with me."

"He is alive," said the hero, "but he can do thee no harm at present. Take him as he is to the king."

The cook said:

"The fight is all over now. Thou mayst be getting ready. When I get the king's daughter, I will have thee as my head-cook."

Then they parted.

The cook went in with the man to the king, and when the king saw the appearance of the man, he praised the cook for his heroism, and said to him:

"I will fulfil my promise to thee. But loose the man, that he may be with us at dinner."

The cook went up to the man and tried to unbind him. But for every knot he untied, there were another seven in the withy band. At length he said that he could not unbind the man.

"Dear me!" said the king, "who could not unbind the man he has bound?"

"It was not he who bound me," said the man. "He could

38

not bind me, and he cannot unbind me. But he who bound me, can unbind me."

"Who is that?" asked the king.

"The Son of the Knight of the Green Vesture, performing heroic deeds which were famed on earth seven years before he was born, and who has fought against our men for the last three days, and who was sleeping in the castle at night — it is he who bound me, and it is he who can unbind me."

Then word was sent to the hero, and he came in. The king looked at him, and when he saw his heroic appearance he went on his knees before him.

When he stood up again, he told him to unbind the man who was bound. The hero caught the knot of the withy band with one hand, and with it lifted the man from the earth. He then let go his hold, and instantly the withy band sprang off the man. As soon as the man got on his feet, he turned to the king, and said:

"Were it not for the talkativeness of the Hen-wife and the Wise Woman's advice to Smooth-brow, there would not have been in the kingdom of the Green Mound a man to run back the Young Son of the Fierce Earl nor to keep Smooth-brow from him. But the hero is worthier of her than I am."

Then Smooth-brow came in, and said to her father:

"Today is the last day of the time thou gavest me to select my choice of a sweetheart. Here is my choice now, and fulfil to me thy promise."

"With all my heart," said the king, "and all that I have, thou shalt have with him."

The cook went back to the cooking, the marriage was arranged, and none in the kingdom saw so comely a pair as Smooth-brow and the Son of the Knight of the Green Vesture.

There was rejoicing and a great feast, and if they have not ceased eating and drinking, they are at it still.

The Swarthy Smith of the Socks

The Swarthy Smith of the Socks had served his time learning smith-craft, but at its close he could not make anything connected with smith-work but socks for ploughs.

He opened a smithy a few miles away from a town, and began sock-making. At that time a fair was held once a month in the nearby town, and as often as it would come round, the Swarthy Smith used to go to it with his old white horse and a cart full of socks. And after selling the socks, he would return home, sound asleep in his cart, leaving the old white horse to find its way as best it could.

One market day he went as usual to the inn, and who met him there but the king's smith. The two soon made one another's acquaintance, and sat down drinking till the liquor went to their heads.

Presently they began to boast, and neither of them would admit that he was not a better smith than the other. To put an end to the wrangle, the king's smith stood up and said to the Swarthy Smith:

"I'll bet three hundred merks that before the next fair I'll make something that nothing you can make within the same time will surpass."

The Swarthy Smith then stood up and answered:

40

"I'll lay another three hundred that you can do nothing of the kind, but that I'll make something to surpass the thing that you will make."

At that the heroes parted, promising to meet at the next fair, having with them the thing they were to make.

At the close of the day the Swarthy Smith returned home in the cart as usual. Next morning he turned out to the smithy and began to make more socks. He kept at them day after day for a year; until the day before the market came round again. That evening a gentleman came to the smithy and said to the Swarthy Smith:

"Have you not started at all at making something with which you are going to win the bet from the king's smith? If you do not begin quickly, be sure you will lose."

The Swarthy Smith replied: "I do not know what you mean — I am not aware that I laid any bet with the king's smith."

"You did," said the gentleman, "I was within hearing, and my own ears heard you lay three hundred merks against him."

"Well then, I will lose, for I never learned to make anything in the world with the exception of socks," said the Swarthy Smith.

"Keep up your courage," said the gentleman, "If you will give me half of what you win, I'll make something for you that will win the bet."

"I'll give you that with all my heart," said the Swarthy Smith.

And without further delay the gentleman set to work. First he made a good lump of a box. After that he placed a large piece of iron in the forge, and in a short time drew it out a deer-hound. And when everything was finished, he put the deer-hound into the box and closed the lid over him.

"Now," said the gentleman, turning to the smith, "when you go away tomorrow with the socks, you will take this box with you, and when you arrive at the fair, the king's smith will be there before you and will come to meet you. If he then asks you to open the box, and show him what is in it, you will tell him that he ought to open his first, because it was he who first laid the bet. Then he will open his box, and a stag will spring out. As soon as you see the stag, open your box, and let out the dog, and I am mistaken if the dog does not win the bet for you."

Then the gentleman bade good evening to the Swarthy Smith and departed.

Next morning the Swarthy Smith went away with his socks and his box in the cart. He reached the fair in good time, and there met the king's smith with a box under his arm. Then everything passed between them as the gentleman had expected. At length the king's smith opened his box, and a fine stag sprang out, and away it went at full speed. Then the Swarthy Smith opened his box, and a handsome deer-hound sprang out and stretched away after the stag, and stopped not until it caught the stag, and left it at the Swarthy Smith's feet.

"Now, I call you to witness," said the Swarthy Smith to the king's smith, "that you have lost your bet."

"I have lost this one, indeed, but perhaps I may win the next," replied the king's smith, while he handed the other every penny of the money wagered.

Then they went to the inn and were not long until they laid another wager such as the last. After that they parted, promising to meet at the next fair, having the machines they would make with them. Then the Swarthy Smith went into the cart, and the white horse took him home.

The first thing he did next morning was to go to the smithy, and hide the three hundred merks in a hole he dug under the door-step. He did not remember anything about the bet, but he continued making socks until the last evening before the fair.

As he was about to stop work that night, who turned into the smithy but the gentleman who had made the deerhound. He greeted the Swarthy Smith, and asked him whether he had yet made the machine with which he was going to win the next bet from the king's smith. But the Swarthy Smith remembered neither that he laid a bet, nor what it was about.

"Well," said the gentleman, "if you promise me half of what you win, and that you will go no more to the inn, I will make you a machine with which you will carry off the bet."

"I promise your first request and also will fulfil the other promise as far as I can," replied the Swarthy Smith.

Then the gentleman set to work. He first made a box, and then a large strong otter in the same way he had made the deer-hound. And when it was ready, he put it in the box, and shut it, and locked the lid over it.

"Now," said he to the Swarthy Smith, "you will take this box with you to the fair and will not open it until the king's smith will first open his. You will win the bet this time yet. But see that you go not to the inn, and that you lay not another bet for fear you lose all you have won. In a few days I will call again at the smithy, and you will give me half of the money you will win." The smith said he would do as he was told, and they parted.

Next day the Swarthy Smith went away with the box to the fair. When he arrived he met the king's smith, but on being asked, refused to open his box first. Then the king's smith went to the water side, and as soon as he opened his box a salmon leapt out into the water, and away he swam. Then the Swarthy Smith opened his own, and the otter sprang out after the salmon, and in a short time seized the salmon, and returned with it in its mouth dropping it at his master's feet.

"I call you to witness," said the Swarthy Smith, "but you

43

have lost your bet."

"I have undoubtedly," replied the king's smith, "and if you come with me to the inn, I'll pay you every penny of it."

"No, I will not, for I have resolved that I will not lay a bet again," said the Swarthy Smith.

"All right," then said the king's smith, and he paid the other smith on the spot.

After a few days who entered the smithy but the gentleman. He waited a while, expecting that the Swarthy Smith would pay unasked what he had earned, but though he should wait to the crack of doom the Swarthy Smith would not mention anything of the kind. At last the gentleman said:

"I have come for my reward. You had better give it to me, and let me go."

But reward or thanks the Swarthy Smith would not give. So the gentleman went away.

A few days after this another gentleman came on horseback to the smithy, and his horse was very lame for want of shoes. After greeting this smith, he said:

"I wish you would shoe my horse, for it is so much in need, and can hardly go another step."

"Is it I!" said the Swarthy Smith. "I never made an article of smith-work except socks for ploughs."

The gentleman replied: "Many a thing a man could make if he had the courage to try. Try you, and I will assist you."

"Very well, then, I will do as well as I can."

The gentleman went out and cut the horse's four feet off below the knees. He took them in to the smith and laid them in the fire. He himself went to the bellow-handle, and the smith was keeping the fire banked up about the feet. After they were a good while in the fire he cried to the Swarthy Smith:

"Out with the heat!"

The smith took hold of the tongs, and with them pulled

T.R.BREHENY

the first foot out of the fire on to the anvil. He then seized the hand hammer, and the gentleman took the sledge hammer, and with a few strokes they shod the foot as neatly as ever a smith did. When they were done with it, they took the other feet, and shod them one by one in the same manner. Then the gentleman cried again to the Swarthy Smith:

"Get you out with the two fore feet, and strike them in their place on the horse."

The Swarthy Smith did that, and the gentleman himself did the same with the two hind feet. In an instant the horse stood up as sound as ever before, shod and ready for the road. Then the gentleman sprang into the saddle, and departed.

As soon as the gentleman went away, the smith entered the house and said to his wife:

'I'll no longer pay wages to rascally smiths, for I can now shoe without them. Come out and help me to shoe the white horse, because I have to go to town soon."

When he had finished what he had to say, he went to the stable and cut the white horse's feet off, and then he took them to the smithy, and put them in the fire. He sent his wife to blow the bellows, while he kept coals over the feet. When he thought they were ready, he drew one out of the anvil, and struck out with the hammer. But the foot up to its middle was nothing but charred bone, and therefore the stroke sent it flying in splinters all over the smithy. The rest of the feet were in the same condition, and so the smith had no choice but to put the poor white horse out of pain at once, and bury the carcass underground as quietly as possible.

A good while after the second gentleman had departed, a third gentleman came to the smith with two old women in his company.

Said he to the Swarthy Smith:

"Will you make for me a young maiden of these old women, and I will give you a good reward for your labour?"

The Swarthy Smith answered:

"Is it I! I have never made anything but socks."

"Will you then give me a while of the smithy and of your assistance?" asked the gentleman.

"Yes, you will get that."

"Come, then, begin work. Many a thing a man could do if he had courage enough to try."

They then put the old women in the fire, and the gentleman went to blow the bellows, and the Swarthy Smith to keep coals on the fire.

When they had given the old women a good heating, they drew them out to the anvil, and then the gentleman began to strike with the sledge hammer, and the smith with the hand hammer, and with one welding heat they made the very handsomest maiden ever beheld. When they had done, the gentleman gave the Swarthy Smith a good reward and departed with the young maiden in his company.

As soon as he had gone, the Swarthy Smith made his way to the house, and said to his wife:

"Have I not news for you? I have just made as handsome a young maiden as you ever saw, of two old wives. Come, and we will make another of your mother and mine, and then we shall have what we never had before, a daughter of our own."

But his wife said:

"Take care so that you will not have the smithing of the white horse over again."

"There is no fear of that," said he, and set to work. He tried to do everything as he saw the gentleman do, but, alas, the result was far worse than the smithing of the white horse. The two old women perished in the fire.

Time passed, and then who called in at the smithy but the first gentleman. After saluting the Swarthy Smith, he said:

"Are you at all disposed to give me, as you promised,

half of the money I earned for you?"

No, the smith was not. He would not as much as thank the gentleman. Then the gentleman became very angry and began to grow so big that the smith was in danger of being flattened between him and the side of the forge. When the Swarthy Smith saw the danger he was in, he took from his pocket a purse which was fastened with thongs, and then he said: "I see that you can make yourself big enough, but if you will now make yourself so small that you can enter this purse, I will give you all the money I owe you."

In an instant the gentleman began to grow smaller and smaller until at last he was so small that he leaped, a little black scrap, into the purse.

As soon as the smith saw this, he drew the thongs and tied them hard and fast about the mouth. He then laid the purse on the anvil, and gave it three strokes of the hammer as hard as he could. The purse burst with such a bang that the smith's wife thought the smithy and all that it contained were blown into the skies. She ran out in terror, and asked what had happened.

"Never mind, if he cheated me over the white horse and the old wives, I have now cheated him out of his life."

The smith continued to make socks and to go with them once a month to the fair, but he became a wise man, and, any time he had need of money, he would take a little from the hoard he had hidden under the threshold of the smithy.

Canobie Dick and Thomas of Ercildoun

Many a long year ago there lived in the Scottish Borders a jolly horse-dealer whom the people called Canobie Dick. He was known for his reckless and fearless ways, which made him much admired and a little dreaded amongst his neighbours.

One night as he rode over Bowden Moor on the west side of the Eildon Hills, close to the spot where Thomas the Rhymer had once met the Fairy Queen, he came across a stranger, wearing the dress of centuries ago.

Dick had with him a brace of horses which he had not been able to sell. And now, to his great surprise, the strange man asked the price of the horses and began bargaining with him. To Dick a chap was a chap, and he would have sold a horse to the Devil himself without minding his cloven hoof and probably would have cheated Old Nick into the bargain.

The stranger then paid the price they agreed on, and all that puzzled Dick in the transaction was that the gold which he received was in unicorns, bonnet-pieces and other ancient coins. These would have been valuable enough to collectors but might turn out rather difficult to dispose of as money.

It was gold, however, and actually Dick managed to get better value for the coins than he perhaps gave to his customer. Satisfied with the deal, he brought horses to the same spot more than once, the stranger always a willing buyer, asking only that Dick should always come by night and alone.

Whether from mere curiosity or whether in the hope of further gain, one night, after again having sold several horses, Dick complained that dry bargains were unlucky, hinting that his customer must live in the neighbourhood, and should, for sheer courtesy, offer him a drink.

"You may see my dwelling if you will," said the stranger, "but if you lose courage at what you see there, you will rue it all your life."

Dick, however, laughed and scorned the warning, and dismounting and tying up his horse, he followed the stranger up a narrow footpath, which led them up the hills towards a curious bluff stuck between the most southern and the central peaks. It was called the Lucken Hare because its shape rather resembled the animal.

Dick was somewhat startled to see his guide enter the hillside by a passage or cavern of which he himself, though well acquainted with the spot, had never known of nor ever seen.

"You may still return," said the guide, looking at him sternly, as if repeating his warning.

But Dick did not weaken, and on they went.

They entered a very long range of stables. In every stall stood a coal-black horse, and by every horse lay a knight in coal-black armour, with a drawn sword in his hand. All were as silent, hook and limb, as if they had been cut out of marble. A great number of torches lent a gloomy lustre to the hall which was very large.

Arriving at the other end Dick saw a sword and a horn lying on an antique table.

"He that shall sound that horn, and draw that sword," said the stranger, "shall, if his heart fail him not, be king

50

over all broad Britain. So speaks the tongue that cannot lie."

At these words Dick realised, not without awe, that he was in the presence of Thomas of Ercildoun, whom they called the Rhymer or True Thomas, as the gift of foretelling the future had been bestowed on him by the Fairy Queen.

"But," continued the stranger, "all depends on courage, and much on your taking the sword or the horn first."

Dick was much disposed to take the sword, but his bold spirit was shaken by the supernatural terrors of the hall, and he feared that to draw the sword first, might give offence to the Powers of the Mountain.

He took the bugle with a trembling hand, and blew a feeble note, but loud enough to produce a terrible answer. Thunder rolled in stunning peals through the immense hall. Horses and men started to life. The steeds snorted, stamped, ground their bits and tossed their heads. The warriors sprang to their feet, clashed their armour, and brandished their swords. Dick's terror was extreme at seeing the whole army, which had been so lately silent as the grave, in uproar, and about to rush on him. He dropped the horn, and made a weak attempt to seize the enchanted sword, but at the same moment a voice pronounced aloud the mysterious words:

Woe to the coward, that ever he was born,
Who did not draw the sword before he blew the horn.

Then a whirlwind of irresistable fury howled through the long hall, bearing the unfortunate Dick clear out of the mouth of the cavern, and tossing him over a steep bank of loose stones where shepherds found him the next morning with just sufficient breath to tell his fearful tale, before he fell back and died.

Donald of the Burthens

Donald was a fire-wood carrier for the house of a nobleman who lived in the country, and it is for that reason he was called Donald of the Burthens.

Donald laboured diligently every day, but his mind was not at rest, he was not satisfied with his condition.

One day, as he was on his way to the nobleman's house, very weary with the burden of the wood that was on his back, a young gentleman met him, and said; "Worthy Donald, you are wearing yourself out. Are you not growing weary of the fire-wood carrying?"

"Yes indeed," he answered, "weary enough, and I should not care though I should get a change of occupation."

Then the young man said to him, "Donald, I am Death, and if you take service with me I'll make a Doctor of you, but on condition that I get you the first time that you cheat me."

Donald accepted the condition, for he would rather do anything than continue carrying fire-wood.

And Death said to him:

"When you'll go to see a sick man, if you see Death standing at his head, you'll take nothing to do with him, for he'll not live, but if Death be standing at his feet, you will take him in hand, for he will live."

Donald did as was requested of him; and he prospered. Every man he said would live, lived, and every person he said would die, died.

Then the king grew very poorly.

Word was sent to Donald, and he came to the castle. But when he went within the king's bedside, he saw Death standing at his head, and would take nothing to do with him. He then asked that the king should be turned in the bed, till his head should be where his feet were, and his feet where his head was. No sooner was this done than the king began to grow better. Donald now saw Death creeping down to the king's head, and he asked that the king should be turned back to his place again. This game went on for some time, till in the end Death got into such a passion that he went away as fast as he could.

When the king grew well, Donald took his departure, but he had not gone far from the castle when Death met him.

"I have you now," said Death, "for you have broken the condition. You have cheated me."

"That is so, without a doubt," said Donald, "but you will allow me respite till I say my prayers?"

And Death granted his request.

Donald then turned to him and said; "I'll never say them all."

Then Death left him in a great rage, vowing he would be even with him yet for all his trickery.

Donald was now left to himself, and Death was not causing him any trouble. Everything continued prosperous with him, and he was growing to great esteem in the country.

Then one day, as Donald was walking on the road alone, a small troop of school children met him. They were very downcast. Donald was a kindly man, and so he went over to ask the children the cause of their trouble.

They answered: "We cannot say our prayer, and our

T.R.BREHENY

Master will punish us." Donald could not stand this. He took a seat at the side of the road, with the small group around him, and taught them their prayer.

No sooner had the children gone than Death came, and said to Donald, "I have you now at all events."

Then said Donald, "You are a wonderful fellow, there's no place where you are not. They tell me that, though you were put in a bottle, you would come out and kill?"

"That is true," said Death.

"I don't believe you, but I have a bottle here, try whether you'll go in."

Death went into the bottle, and Donald knocked the cork in tight, commanding at the same time, "Stop you there."

He then went away with the bottle, and threw it into a loch. Once more he was free.

However, not long after, the bottle came to land where it was broken. Death then got at large, and never halted till he had put an end to Donald.

The Son of the
Strong Man of the Wood

Once upon a time there lived a big man whom the people called the Strong Man of the Wood. This man's employment was hunting deer, and bringing home fuel for the fire.

One day he went to cut down a large oak tree which he had seen the day before in the wood. The tree was bending over, and it fell on him, bruising him dreadfully; but the man was strong, and succeeded in dragging himself out from under it. When he rose up on his feet, he took hold of the tree by its trunk, and he dragged it between root and top home with him.

As soon as he threw it off his shoulder at the door, he fell.

His wife came out, and when she saw how he was, she helped him in, and sat him on the bed-side. He then drew a great sigh, and said that he was hurt to death. His fist was closed, and when he opened it, there was an acorn in his hand. He looked at it, and then handed it to his wife, saying:

"I am going to die, but thou shalt plant this acorn in the midden before the door. Thou art going to have a son, and on the night when he comes into the world, the seedling of the acorn shall be coming in sight through the ground. Thou shalt nourish your son on thy knee with the milk of thy breast until he becomes so strong, that he can take the tree which shall grow from the acorn out of its base and roots."

After saying this, the man lay down and rose no more.

When the time came the woman had a son, and as soon as he was born, she told the midwife to go out and see if there was a seedling from the acorn. And, indeed, the seedling had broken through the ground.

She took her son, and nourished him for seven years on her knee. Then she led him to the tree, and told him that he should try to take the tree from its root. The boy attacked the tree, and gave it a terrible shaking and pulling, but it was so firmly rooted in the earth that he did not move it.

When his mother saw that he could not uproot the tree, she carried her son into the house, and nursed him for seven more years. Then she took him out to the tree, and told him that he was to see whether he or the tree was the stronger now. He took hold of the trunk of the tree, and pulled it dreadfully, but it was rooted so firmly in the ground that he did not manage to pull it out.

When his mother saw that again he could not uproot the tree, she carried her son into the house, and nursed him for another seven years. Then she took him out to the tree again, and told him to try and find out which of them was stronger — himself or the tree. The boy leapt over to the tree took hold of it with his two hands, shook it, and made it shake, and with three or four pulls had it out by its foundation and roots. He then began at its top, broke and smashed it, until he made firewood of it, and left it in a heap at the door.

Then his mother said:

"I have nursed thee long enough now, and thou art thoroughly able to earn a livelihood for thyself in future. Come in, and I will bake for thee a bannock, thou shalt have it with my blessing, and then thou shalt go away to win a fortune for thyself."

58

The boy took the bannock from his mother and departed.

He travelled onwards to see whether he should happen to come on a place where he might get employment. At last he arrived at a fine large steading with more corn-stacks about it than he ever saw together. He thought that he might get work in the place, and took his way straight to the house.

He knocked at the door, asking to see the master. The master came, and the big lad explained that he was looking for work.

"Thy appearance will do," said the master. "I have enough work, and I do not know why thou shouldst not get it. Canst thou thrash?"

"Yes," replied the lad.

"Thou art tired," said the master. "Look around tonight, and tomorrow, early in the morning, thou shalt begin thrashing."

"Where shall I begin?"

"In the barn, for there is as much corn there as will keep two men thrashing for six weeks, let them work ever so well. When that is done, there is behind the barn a large yard full of corn-stacks, and every straw of them is to be thrashed."

The barn and the stack-yard were built on a brae above the house of the farmer. When the lad had got his food, he went up to the barn to see those who were thrashing there. He went in, and after having looked at them for a while, he took hold of the flail which one of them had, and said:

"The flails you have are worthless. When I begin tomorrow you shall see the flail which I will have."

He then went away to the wood to cut a flail for himself, and when it was ready its handle resembled the mast of a ship.

At that time the rule was that the men-servants must work from star to star, which means from the setting of the stars to their rising. This the big lad knew, and therefore he rose early in the morning and commenced thrashing even before

59

the last star had left the sky. He began thrashing the mow which was in the barn, laid it in one end, and as he was advancing, he was sending the roof out of the building. He kept on at that rate until there was not a straw unthrashed on the floor before breakfast time arrived.

After he had got his breakfast, he turned out again. He took his way to the stack-yard, carried with him a stack under each arm and one between his two hands, placed them in the barn, and thrashed them. He kept working away in that manner until there was not a stack in the yard unthrashed before dinner time had come. The whole farm was then white with straw, and the walls of the barn nearly full of grain.

Then he went to look for the farmer. The farmer met him on the way, wondering greatly where all the straw came from. But he uttered not a syllable to the big lad. Then the lad asked what he would do now.

"Thou shalt go thrash in the barn," said the farmer.

"There is no thrashing left which I can do."

"What dost thou say! There is as much thrashing in the barn as will keep two men at work for six weeks, let them work ever so well."

"No. There is not a straw on the farm — in the barn or stack-yard — that is not already thrashed."

The farmer did not know what to say to this, but he told the lad to go in and get his dinner, while he himself went to the barn to see whether the lad told him the truth or not.

He reached the barn, and when he saw the appearance that everything before him had, the roof sent out of the barn, the straw scattered everywhere, and every stack in the yard thrashed, he was seized with great fear, and what caused him the greatest terror was the flail which the big lad used.

He returned to the house trembling with fear, and took a back road rather than meet the big lad when he came out from his meal. But the big lad noticed him, and took his way straight to meet him. He asked of him what would he go to do? The farmer knew not very well what answer he should give, but what he said was:

"Since thou hast worked so well before dinner time, thou hadst better take a rest for this evening."

Then the big lad said:

"Thou hast seen my work now, and thou knowest what I can do. I must get more food for my dinner than I am getting."

"How much must thou get?"

"A quarter of a chalder of meal in brose one day, and a quarter of a chalder in bannocks with the carcass of a two-year-old stot another day."

"Thou shalt get that," said the farmer, trembling with fear.

The farmer went in, and he told the people in the house what food they had to make ready for the big lad every day in future.

The farmer and the wise men who were about him thought of the matter, and saw that the big lad would ruin the farm in food unless they could find out a method of destroying him or of sending him away.

Now there lived a very old man on the farm whom people called Big Angus of the Rocks, and one of the men said:

"If Big Angus does not know what we should do with him, there is no other man in the place who can tell us."

The farmer sent for Big Angus. Angus came, and the farmer told him every particular about the giant who came on them — how he thrashed the corn, and the sort of flail with which he worked.

"Alas!" said Angus, "he has come at last! I heard my grandfather talking of him when I was a little boy. He was as old as I am at this day, while he was telling how it was said that this place would be ruined yet by a giant, and I have no doubt at all but that it is he who has come here."

"Canst thou think of any method by which he can be destroyed?"

"The only method I can imagine is this: thou shalt tell him to open a big well in the middle of the field over yonder, and go so deep that the water will meet him. It is a deep sandy bottom, and he must go a great depth before he can reach the spring. But when he will reach it, have every man who can handle a shovel about thee, and when he will happen to stoop at the bottom of the hole, let every man be equal to two men driving the stuff in on the top of him. But if you see him stand up, let every man of you run away; for if he will get his head raised, he will be out in spite of you and kill you."

The farmer consented to this.

That same night he sent for the big lad. He came, and the farmer told him that the water was getting exceedingly scarce, and that he therefore wanted to open a well in the field over yonder.

"Right enough," said the lad.

"Thou shalt begin it as thy first morning's work tomorrow," said the farmer.

When daylight came, the big lad began to open the well. The men also were early on the ground. They went out with the farmer to watch the big lad, to see how he was getting on with the hole. When they got a sight of him, only the top of his head was above the ground, and a great heap of stuff was being thrown out by him. They became afraid that they would be too late, but they were in good time at the hole. The farmer stood at the mouth of the hole, and when the lad stooped, he cried to the men to begin. They began to put the stuff in upon him as nimbly as they could ply a shovel. But they were not long at that work when the big lad stood up in the hole, shook his hand, and shouted:

"Whish!"

The farmer cried to his men to run away, and every man of

them went off as fast as his feet could carry him.

The big lad finished the hole.

He then went up to the farmer's house. As he approached it, he was astonished that there was not a man to be seen about the farm. He reached the door, and put his hand on the bar, but the door was so strongly shut on the inside that it would not open for him. He then laid his palm against the bar, and pushed it stronger than he wished. The bar broke, and the door opened. He went in, and found the farmer crouching under the table and trembling.

The farmer came out on the floor, and asked the big lad if he had finished the hole. The lad said that he had.

"But why," said he, "didst thou not send a man to keep away the rooks? They nearly put out my eyes, scratching the sand for worms. But what shall I go to do now?"

"Oh, go and get thy dinner," said the farmer.

The big lad went as he was told.

When he had gone, the farmer sent for the old man again, and said to him:

"Yon plan will do no good. He made the hole more than thirty feet in depth, I had every man about the place round the hole, and when he was stooping at the bottom, we poured stuff in on the top of him, but he stood up in the hole, and shouted whish! and then we fled.

"In a short time he came home after us. He went to the door, and though it was shut and barred, he sent it in before him with one push of his hand. He came in then, and forsooth said to me, why did I not send a man to keep away the rooks, because they had nearly put out his eyes scratching the sand in on the top of him while he was cleaning the bottom of the hole!"

"Oh, then," said Big Angus, "we will try another plan with him."

"What plan is that?"

"Send him to plough the Crooked Ridge of the Field of

the Dark Lake. Out of that never came man or beast that did not plough there to the going down of the sun."

"We will try that plan with him," said the farmer.

He sent for the big lad, and said to him that he was to plough in the Crooked Ridge of the Field of the Dark Lake.

"Very right," said the lad. "I will do that."

Early in the morning he made ready for the ploughing. He carried the plough with him on his shoulder, he had the two horses by the reins after him, and reached the Field of the Dark Lake. He thrust the plough in the end of the Crooked Ridge, and yoked the horses. There was a large tree in the middle of the Ridge, and he said to himself:

"I will open the ground in line with the tree."

Then he began to plough.

He was getting on well during the day but at the going down of the sun he heard a dreadful plunge in the lake. He gave a look, and saw a big uncouth object moving in the water, but paid no attention to it, and kept ploughing away as he was doing before. As soon as the sun went out of sight the beast came to land, and swept up the shore of the lake to the farthest end of the Crooked Ridge. It then put about, and walked towards the team of horses in the very furrow in which the big lad was ploughing with them. The big lad kept going forward with the horses, and they met the beast near the tree that was in the middle of the Ridge. The big lad cried to the beast that it was to keep back, otherwise it would see what would happen to it. But the beast gave no heed to him, opened its mouth, and swallowed one of the horses alive and whole.

"That will do," said the big lad. "I will make thee put the horse out as quickly as thou didst swallow it."

He then let go the plough and went up close to the beast. They had terrible bouts of wrestling, but in the end the big lad was above the beast.

"Put out the horse now," said the lad.

64

But the beast did not heed him.

"I will make thee put it out," said he again.

He then took hold of the beast by the tail, dragged him to the tree, pulled the tree out of its root, and belaboured the beast with it, until only as much of the top of the tree was left as the lad could hold in his hand. Then he said:

"Wilt thou put out the horse now?"

The beast did not heed him yet.

"Well," said the lad, "I will make thee do the work of the one thou hast eaten, at any rate."

The other horse had broken the traces and ran home. When it reached the house, and the farmer saw the scared appearance of it, he said:

"Oh, there is no doubt that the big lad and the other horse are dead now! The Water-horse of the Dark Lake has put an end to him at last!"

But the big lad was about his own business. He tied the beast in the plough and began ploughing with it, and before he stopped, there was not a furrow in the Crooked Ridge that he did not turn over. When he was done, he went home, holding the big horse by the head.

He reached the farmer's door and cried to him to come out. But no man answered, for everybody on the farm had fled into hiding as soon as they had seen him and the horse coming. He then gave deafening blows to the door, and at last the farmer came out, trembling with fear.

The big lad asked him what would he do tomorrow.

"Oh, thou shalt plough," said the farmer, with a tremulous voice.

"I have no ploughing I can do."

"What dost thou say? There is as much land in the Crooked Ridge as would keep a pair of horses ploughing for six weeks."

"There is not. I ploughed every furrow before I stopped."

"And didst thou notice anything which troubled thee

while thou wert at work?"

"I noticed nothing but a nasty thing of an ugly beast that came out of the Lake and ate one of my horses. I tried to make it put the horse out, but the beast would not heed me. I then put it in the plough, and ploughed every furrow of the Crooked Ridge with it, but the beast has not put out the horse yet."

"And where is the beast?"

"It is here, at the door."

"Oh, let it go! Let it go! Let it away!"

"I will not until I get the horse back."

The lad then turned to the beast and laid it on its back. He drew his own big knife, split up the beast's belly with it, and took out the horse alive and whole.

He then said to the farmer:

"I do not know what to do with the beast unless I put it in the hole in the middle of the field, and if there was no water in it before, there will be then."

He dragged the beast over to the field, threw it head foremost in the hole, put earth in on top of it, and left it there.

Again the farmer sent for Big Angus of the Rocks. Angus came, and said to the farmer:

"What news hast thou now?"

"I have only poor news. Yon attempt did no good. I sent him to plough the Crooked Ridge; while he was ploughing a fearful beast came out of the lake and ate one of the horses. He seized the beast, tied it to the plough, and before he stopped, ploughed with the beast every furrow of the Ridge. He then took it home, holding it by the end of a halter, he threw it down at the door, and took the horse alive and whole out of its belly. Then he drew the beast by the tail after him, and threw it head foremost in the hole. And now I do not think that we can fight him any longer. We may as well run away, and leave the place to the big lad."

"We shall give him another trial yet."

"What trial is that?"

"Say to him that the meal has failed on thee, and that thou shalt not have a morsel of food for him until he himself returns from the Mill. Thou shalt send him away with a sled of corn to the Mill of Leckan. Thou shalt cause him to make haste, in order that he may work in the Mill all night, and I warrant thee that the Big Brownie of the Mill of Leckan will not let him home more than any other man. But if he will, and you see the lad coming, all of you, small and large, young and old, may run away, for he cannot be destroyed, and he will ruin the place at any rate."

The farmer sent for the big lad, and said to him that the meal had failed, and that he would not have a morsel of food for him until he came with meal from the Mill.

"Take with thee any one of the horses thou pleasest and the big sled, and fill it with sacks of corn, and thou shalt come home as soon as thou canst. Thou must work all night in the Mill in order that you mayst be back early in the morning."

"Very right," said the big lad; "I will do that."

He went away with the grain without any delay, and reached the Mill in the dusk. The miller had ceased grinding, and the mill was shut. He loosened the horse out of the sled, and let him go to pasture. Then he went to the miller's house, and shouted at the door for the miller to get up, because he had come with a sled of grain, and must get it ground that night.

"It matters not who thou art, or whence thou hast come, but there is not a man on the face of the earth for whom I would open the mill any more this night."

"Oh, thou must get up. I am in a hurry, and the grain must be ground tonight."

"Hurry or no hurry, I never saw a man for whom I would go to the mill tonight."

"If thou do not go, give me the key, and I will go myself."

"Well, if thou enter it, thou shalt not come out of it alive."

"I have no fear at all; give me the key."

The miller gave him the key, and he went away to the mill. He carried the grain in, made a great fire of seeds and peats, placed a layer of corn on the kiln, hardened the corn, and put it in the hopper. He then set the mill going, ground as much of the oats as he dried, riddled the meal, and at last began to knead bannocks, for he was very hungry. When they were kneaded, he put them on the kiln to bake.

While he was baking and turning them, he noticed an uncouth object coming in sight in a corner of the kiln. He called on the thing to keep back, but the thing heeded him not. It stretched out its paw and took away one of the bannocks.

"Do not do that again," said the big lad.

But the thing did not heed him. In a short time it again stretched out its paw, and took another bannock.

"Do that once more, and I will make the bannocks dear to thee," said the big lad.

The thing in the corner paid little attention to the threat, and it took a third bannock.

"Well," said the big lad, "if thou give no heed of thine own free will, I will make thee put back what thou hast taken with thee."

Then he gave a great heavy leap, ending in a fall, and was right on top of the thing. They went in each other's grips, and wrestled dreadfully. With a turn or two they threw down the kiln, they shattered the mill, and people far and near heard the terrible deafening noise. The miller heard it in his bed, and it put him in such fear that he wrapped the bed-clothes about him and crept down to the foot of the bed. His wife, shrieking, leapt over on to the floor, and went on all fours under the bed.

At long last the big lad subdued the thing which begged to be let go, but the big lad said he would not let it go in that way.

"Thou shalt not get away until thou repair the mill, and put up the kiln with the bannocks on it as thou didst find them."

Then he gave the thing further terrible bruisings until the thing cried:

"Let me go, and I will do everything that thou biddest me!"

"I will not let thee go, but thou must do my bidding while I have a hold of thee."

Then the thing began to repair the mill, and in a short time he put everything in its own place as it was formerly.

"Let me go now, for everything is as I found it," said the thing.

The big lad gave a look, and saw that the three bannocks were not on the kiln, and he said that everything was not as it was.

"Where are the bannocks thou didst take with thee?"

He now gave the thing further dreadful blows and bruisings until it cried:

"Let me go, and thou shalt find the bannocks in the fire-place."

"I will not let thee go, but go thou and find them for me."

The thing went, the big lad having a hold of him and found the bannocks.

"Put them now on the kiln where thou didst find them," said the big lad. The thing did that, and the big lad gave it the next bruisings. The thing again cried to let it go, and that it would leave the mill, and never trouble it after that night.

"Well, since thou hast promised that, I will let thee go," said the big lad, and gave it a shove out through the door. The thing gave three horrible screams and went away. The miller heard the screams, and his wife uttered a piercing cry from under the bed.

When the thing had gone, the big lad began to eat the bannocks, and when he had eaten enough, he dried and ground

70

the remainder of the grain. He then riddled the meal, put it in the sacks, and put the sacks on the sled. He now had everything ready; and therefore he locked the door of the mill, and went away with the key.

He reached the miller's house, and shouted at the door, but nobody answered him. He shouted again, and heard the miller answering with a faint voice within. The big lad asked him to open the door because he had come back with the key.

"Oh!" said the miller, "be off! be off! and take with thee the key along with the other things."

"It is I, let me in," said the big lad.

But the miller did not answer him at all, so he pushed the door before him, and went in.

"Here," said he, "is the key for thee, for I have ground the grain, and I am going home."

When the miller heard that the grain was ground, he took his head out of the bedclothes, and looked at the man.

"Oh, how art thou alive after being in the mill all night!"

"Pooh! thou mayest go to the mill, and stay in it all night now! I have made the thing that was in it run away, and it shall never more trouble thee or any other man."

"Oh, wife art thou hearing yon?" asked the miller. But his wife answered not a word. The big lad asked where she was. The miller replied that she fled and hid herself under the bed when she heard the noise in the mill. The big lad gave a look under the bed, and drew her out on the floor, but she was dead for her heart had ceased beating from fear.

Then the big lad left the miller's house and started home.

There was a brae above the mill, and because the horse began to stop in the ascent, he gave it a blow with the back of his hand. Alas, the blow was so heavy that it broke the horse's shoulder, and the horse fell on the road. The big lad was very sorry for what had happened, but there was no help for it. He loosed the horse out of the sled, threw it on the top of the sacks, and went to draw the sled himself. He set off cheerily with it until he reached the top of the brae.

The farmer had put a watch on every road by which the big lad could return. At last one of the watchers saw him from afar, dragging the sled after him, the horse on top of the sacks. The man threw off his footgear and every bit of clothing which would hinder his running, and ran away as fast as he could until he reached the farmer's house.

The farmer asked him whether he saw a sight of the big lad.

"Did I see a sight of him? Tis I who saw a sight of him! He would not wait for the horse, but threw it on the top of the sacks, and he himself is drawing the sled after him with great speed."

"Oh, then we must go away, for he will kill us all and will ruin the place at any rate."

Then they went away, and left the place to the big lad.

He arrived in a short time. He took the horse down off the top of the sled, and put the sacks in. He looked round, but there was not a man to be seen about the farm. He searched every hole and corner where he could think a man might be hidden, but found none. At last he understood that everyone on the farm had fled, leaving it to him.

He then thought that he would go for his mother, and that he would take her to the fine place which was now his. He found her at the foot of the wood, and told her of the great good luck he had had, and that he had come for her to go and stay with him. The mother said:

"I am old now, and it is too far for me to walk."

"Well, mother, it shall not be so. Thou dist take a long time carrying me, and I will carry thee thus far now."

With that he lifted his mother on his back, and did not let go of her until he reached the place which was now his.

There they lived in plenty and ease, and if they are alive, they are still there.

Mac Iain Direach

There was once a king and a queen, and they had one son. But the queen died, and the king married another wife. The name of the first queen's son was Mac Iain Direach. He was a handsome lad, and fond of hunting. There was no bird at which he would cast his arrow that he would not fell, and he would kill the deer and the roes at a great distance from him. There was no day when he would go out with his bow and quiver that he would not bring home some game.

One day, however, he was out hunting, and he got no game at all. Then a blue falcon came past him, and he shot an arrow at the bird, but only a feather dropped from its wing. He picked up the feather, and put it in his hunting bag.

When he came home with it, his stepmother said:

"Where is thy game today?" and he put his hand into the hunting bag, took out the feather, and gave it to her.

At once the queen knew that the feather came from no ordinary bird, and decided that she must get possession of it, even if it meant using her magic powers.

So she said to Iain: "I am setting it as crosses and as spells on thee; thou be not without a pool in thy shoe, and that thou be wet, cold and soiled, until thou gettest for me the bird from which that feather came."

And Mac Iain Direach went away as fast as he could to

73

seek the bird from which the feather came. He travelled long and he travelled far, looking for the falcon, but he could not find it. Night was falling, and the little fluttering birds were going from the bush tops, from tuft to tuft, and to the briar roots, going to rest; and though they were, Iain was not until the night came blind and dark, and he went and crouched at the root of a briar.

Then who should come his way but Gille Mairtean, the fox, and he said:

'Thou art down in the mouth Mac Iain Direach, thou camest on a bad night. I have but one wether's trotter and a sheep's cheek, but needs must do with it."

They kindled a fire, and they roasted the flesh, and they ate the wether's trotter and the sheep's cheek. In the morning Gille Mairtean said to the king's son:

"Oh son of Iain Direach, the falcon thou seekest is by the great Giant of the Five Heads, and the Five Humps, and the Five Throttles, and I will show thee where his house is. It is my advice that thou be nimble and ready to do each thing that is asked of thee, and each thing that is trusted to thee, and be very good to his birds, and it well may be that he will trust thee with the falcon to feed. And when thou gettest the falcon to feed, be right good to it, till thou gettest a chance. When the giant is not at home, run away with the bird, but take care that not as much as one feather touches any one thing that is in the house. If it does touch something, it will not go well with thee."

"I'll take care of that," answered Iain, and went to the giant's house. When he arrived, he knocked at the door, and the giant shouted:

"Who is there?"

"It is I," replied Mac Iain Direach, "one coming to see if thou hast need of a lad."

"What work canst thou do?" asked the giant.

Said Iain: "I can feed birds and swine, and feed and milk

74

TR.BREHENY

a cow or goats or sheep."

"It is the like of thee that I want," said the giant.

Then the giant came out, settled wages on Mac Iain Direach, and he took good care of everything that the giant had, and he was very kind to the hens and the ducks. And the giant took notice how well the lad was doing, and he said that his table was so good since Iain had come, that he would rather have one hen of those which he got now, than two of those he used to get before.

"My lad is so good that I begin to think I may trust him with the falcon to feed."

So the giant gave the falcon to Mac Iain Direach to feed, and the lad took exceedingly good care of the bird.

When the giant saw how well Iain looked after the falcon, he thought that he might entrust the bird to him when he himself was away from home.

One day the giant did go away, thinking that all was well with his precious bird, but Mac Iain Direach thought that the time had come to run away with the falcon.

He seized the bird, and when he opened the door, the falcon saw the light and spread its wings, so that the point of one of the feathers on one of its wings touched the door-post, and the door-post let out a screech.

At that the giant came running home, and he caught Iain, and he took the falcon from him, saying:

"I will not give thee my falcon, unless thou wilt get me the White Sword of Light that the Big Women of Dhiurradh are guarding."

With that the giant sent Iain away.

And again he walked and he walked until he met with Gille Mairtean. And the fox said:

"Thou art down in the mouth, Mac Iain Direach. Thou didst not, and thou wilt not do as I tell thee. Bad is the night on which thou hast come — I have but one wether's trotter and one sheep's cheek, but needs must do with that."

They kindled a fire, and they made ready the wether's trotter and the sheep's cheek, and they took their food, and slept. On the next day Gille Mairtean said:

"We will go to the side of the ocean."

They started walking, and eventually reached the side of the ocean when Gille Mairtean said:

"I will grow into a boat, and go thou on board of her, and I will take thee over to Dhiurradh, and the Seven Big Women. Then go and ask to be a servant with them, and when they demand to know what thou canst do, say to them that thou art good at brightening iron and steel, gold and silver, and that thou canst make them bright, clear, and shiny. Then they may trust thee with the White Sword of Light, and when thou gettest a chance, run away with it, but take care that the sheath does not touch a thing on the inner side of the house, or it will make a screech, and things will not go well with thee."

Then Gille Mairtean grew into a boat, and Iain went on board of her, and soon he landed in Dhiurradh. He leapt on the shore, and went to take service with the Seven Big Women. He reached the place where they were living, and he knocked at their door.

The Seven Big Women came out, and asked what he was seeking.

"I am looking for work," said he. "I could brighten, or make clear and shiny, gold, silver, iron or steel."

And the women answered: "We have need for the likes of thee." And they set wages on him.

For six weeks the lad was very diligent, putting everything in good order, and the Big Women noticed it. They kept saying to each other:

"This is the best lad we have ever had. We may trust him with the White Sword of Light."

They gave him the sword to keep in order, and he was taking exceedingly good care of it. Then when one day the

77

Big Women were not at home, he thought this was the time for him to run away with the White Sword of Light. He put it into the sheath, and he raised it on his shoulder, but when he was going out at the door the point of the sheath touched the lintel, and the lintel made a screech.

Immediately the Big Women came running home and took the sword from Iain, saying:

"We will not give thee our White Sword of Light, unless thou wilt get for us the Yellow Filly of the King of Eirinn."

Mac Iain Direach went to the side of the ocean where Gille Mairtean met him and said:

"Thou art down in the mouth, Mac Iain Direach. Thou didst not, and thou wilt not do as I tell thee. I have tonight but one wether's trotter and one sheep's cheek, but needs must do with it."

They kindled a fire, and they roasted the flesh, and they were satisfied. On the next day Gille Mairtain said to Iain:

"I will grow into a barque, and go thou on board of her, and I will go to Eirinn with thee, and when we reach Eirinn, go thou to the house of the king, and ask to be a stable lad with him. And when thou gettest that, be nimble and ready to do all that is to be done, and keep the horses and the harness in right good order, till the king trust the Yellow Filly to thee. And when thou gettest a chance to run away with it, take care when thou art taking the filly out that no bit of the horse touches anything that is on the inner side of the gate, except the soles of its feet, or else things will not go well with thee."

Then Gille Mairtean transformed himself into a barque. Iain went on board, and off the barque sailed for Eirinn. When they reached the shore Mac Iain Direach leapt on land, and went to the house of the king. When he reached the gate, the gatekeeper asked where he was going. Said the lad:

"I am going to see if the king has need of a stable boy."

Then the gatekeeper let him pass, and he knocked at the

door of the king's house.

At that the king came out, asking:

"What art thou seeking here?"

Said he:

"With your leave, I came to see if you had need of a stable lad."

Then aked the king:

"What canst thou do?"

Said he:

"I can clean and feed horses, and clean the silver work and the steel work, and make them shiny."

The king then settled wages on him, and the lad went to the stable, and put everything in good order. He took good care of the horses, fed them well, and kept them clean. Their skin was looking sleek, and the silver work and the steel work shiny, and the king had never seen them so well in order before. And he said:

"This is the best stable lad I have ever had, I may trust the Yellow Filly with him."

Then the king gave the Yellow Filly to Mac Iain Direach to keep, and the lad took very great care of the horse. He kept her clean until her skin was so sleek and slippery, and she so swift that she ran like the very wind. The king had never seen her do so well.

One day the king went to the hunting hill, and Iain thought that was the very time to run away with the Yellow Filly. He saddled her, and when he took her out of the stable and went through the gate, she gave a swish with her tail, and the point of her tail touched the post of the gate, and it let out a screech.

The king came running and took the filly from Iain, saying:

"I will not give thee the Yellow Filly, unless thou wilt get for me the daughter of the king of France."

Mac Iain Direach needs must go, and when he was by the side of the ocean Gille Mairtean met him, and said:

"Thou art down in the mouth, Mac Iain Direach. Thou

79

didst not, and thou wilt not do as I ask thee. We must now go to France."

Then Gille Mairtean transformed himself into a ship, and Iain Mac Direach went on board of her, and Gille Mairtean sailed to France with him.

When they landed on a rocky coast, the fox said to Iain:

"Go up to the king's house, and say that thy skipper has been lost, and thy ship thrown on the shore."

Mac Iain Direach went to the king's house, and knocked at the door. Somebody came out to see who was there, and the lad told his tale, and was taken inside.

The king asked him whence he came, and what he was doing here.

"Your Majesty," said Iain, "a great storm came on us; my skipper is lost, and my ship thrown on dry land. There, driven up on the face of a rock, I do not know how to float my ship again."

Then the king and the queen, and their whole family went to the shore to see the ship. When they were looking at it, sweet music began on board, and the king of France's daughter asked to go on board to see the musical instruments.

She went with Mac Iain Direach, and when they were in to one part of the ship, the music would be in another. But at last they heard the music on the upper deck, and they followed it.

That very moment wind caught the sails, and the ship was out in the ocean, and out of sight of land.

Then the princess said:

"Bad is the trick thou has played on me. Where art thou going with me?"

"I am going with thee to Eirinn," said the lad, "to give thee as wife to the king of Eirinn, so that I may get from him the Yellow Filly, to give her to the Big Women of Dhiurradh, that I may get from them the White Sword of Light, to give to the great Giant of the Five Heads, and Five Humps and Five Throttles, that I may get from him the Blue Falcon to

80

take home to my stepmother, the queen, so that I may be free from the bad spells she has laid upon me."

Then said the king of France's daughter:

"I would rather be a wife to thee."

And when they came to the shore in Eirinn, Gille Mairtean transformed himself into a fine woman, saying to Mac Iain Direach:

"Leave thou the king of France's daughter here till we return, and I will go with thee to the King of Eirinn."

Iain went with Gille Mairtean in the shape of a pretty maiden. When the king of Eirinn saw them coming he went out to meet them, leading the Yellow Filly with a golden saddle on her back, and a silver bridle.

Then Iain went away with the filly to where the king of France's daughter was waiting for him. The king of Eirinn was well pleased with his bride but little did he know it was Gille Mairtean, the fox, he had got.

It was, however, not long before the fox — back to his natural shape — sprang on the king, bit him, and ran away. Rejoining Iain and the king of France's daughter by the side of the ocean, he said:

"I will transform myself into a ship, and go thou on board of her, with the Yellow Filly, and I will take thee to Diurradh."

Soon the ship was there, and Iain put in the Yellow Filly first, and he himself and the king of France's daughter went in after, and off they sailed to Diurradh. As they went ashore, Gille Mairtean said:

"Leave thou the Yellow Filly here, and the king's daughter till thou return, and I will transform myself into a filly, and will go with thee to the Big Women of Diurradh." Gille Mairtean then went in the shape of a filly with the golden saddle on her back, and the silver bridle on her head.

When the Big Women saw them coming, they presented Mac Iain Direach with the White Sword of Light. In return Iain left the filly with the women. Then he returned with the White Sword of Light to the king of France's daughter, and the Yellow Filly.

And the Big Women believing that they now had the Yellow Filly of the king of Eirinn, were in a great hurry to ride it.

They mounted the filly, one after the other, until all seven were mounted on what really was Gille Mairtean's back. Then one of the women gave a whip to Gille Mairtean, and he ran and raced backwards and forwards through the moors, with the whole lot of them. At last they went bounding high to the top of a mountain, where he moved his front towards the crag, digging in his hooves, and bolting high into the air, he tossed the Seven Big Women into the sea below.

This done, he rejoined Mac Iain Direach and the king of France's daughter, waiting with the Yellow Filly and the White Sword of Light.

Said the fox:

"I will now transform myself into a boat, and go thyself and the daughter of the king of France on board, and take with you the Yellow Filly and the White Sword of Light, and I will take thee to the mainland."

It was no quicker said than done.

When they reached the shore, Gille Mairtean took on his own shape, saying to Iain:

"Leave thou the king of France's daughter, the Yellow Filly and the White Sword of Light here, and I will transform myself into the Sword. Then take me to the giant, and give me to him for the Falcon.

Then the fox transformed himself into the Sword, and Iain took him to the giant. When the giant saw him coming, he put the Blue Falcon into a basket, and gave it to Mac Iain Direach, who returned with it to the king of France's daughter, the Yellow Filly and the White Sword of Light.

The giant held Gille Mairtean in his hand, believing that it was the White Sword of Light of the Big Women of Diurradh.

He began fencing and slashing with it, till at last Gille Mairtean bent himself, and cut off the five heads of the giant in one single sweep.

The fox then went back to Iain, and said:

"Mac Iain Direach put the saddle of gold on the filly, and the silver bridle on her head, and ride her, taking the king of France's daughter at the back. Carry the White Sword of Light with its back against thy nose, or else, when thy stepmother will see thee, she will bewitch thee with her deadly glance, and thou will fall, a stick of firewood. But if the back of the sword is against thy nose, and its edge to her, when she tries to bewitch thee, she herself will fall down — nothing but a stick of firewood."

And Iain did as the fox told him, and when he faced the queen, she looked at him with a deadly bewitching eye, but it was she who fell down, nothing but a dry stick of wood.

Now Iain was free from fear, with the most beautiful girl beside him. He also had the Yellow Filly, as swift as the wind, and the Blue Falcon which would keep him in plenty when he was out hunting, with the White Sword of Light to ward off all foes.

Mac Iain Direach was truly happy, and he said to Gille Mairtean:

"Thou art welcome to go through my ground, and take any beast thou dost desire. I will give word to my servants that they do not let an arrow harm thee, and that they do not kill thee, nor any of thy kind."

To that Gille Mairtean answered:

"Keep thou thy herds to thyself. There is many a one that has wethers and sheep, and I will get plenty of flesh in other place without bothering thee."

And the fox gave a blessing to Iain, and went away.

Then a great marriage feast was held, and Mac Iain Direach and the daughter of the king of France lived happily ever after.

And that brought the tale to an end.

The Importance of Fairy Names

A name is an important thing, and the fairies set great store by theirs. Many tales speak of the care with which the fairies will conceal their names from humans. But should by accident or cunning a human stumble on the name of a fairy, he is lucky indeed, for then the fairy is in his power, and will have to yield to the human's demands. This usually makes the fairy very angry.

Habetrot

There was once a Selkirkshire lassie who was so idle that her mother could never teach her to spin. She was a merry, pretty lass, but her delight was to scramble about in the woods and hills and sit by the burns, and though her mother begged and scolded, she could never get her to sit long enough at her wheel to do any good there. At last her mother lost patience, and she took seven heads of lint and gave them to the lassie.

"See here, you idle little thing," she said. "You'll spin these seven heads into yarn in three days, or I'll give you a good spanking you'll not forget so soon."

The lassie knew her mother meant what she said, and she sat down to work. Her soft little hands were blistered with the harsh lint, and her lips were quite sore with licking the thread. But for two days she worked hard and just finished half a head.

She cried herself to sleep that night, for she knew she could never finish the rest of her task in one day. So the next morning she gave it up and went out into the sunshine and clear air. She wandered up and she wandered down until she came to a little knoll with a stream running past it, and by the stream, sitting on a self-bored stone, was an old woman spinning. She looked up as the lassie came near, and her looks were friendly enough. But her lips were so long and thick that the lassie had never seen the like.

The lassie smiled at her and came up. "Good day to you, goodwife," she said. "You're a grand spinner, but why are you so long-lipped?".

"Spinning the thread, my hinnie," said the old woman kindly.

"I should be doing that too," said the lassie. "But it's no good, I can't do it in time."

"Fetch me your lint, my hinnie, and I'll spin it for you," said the old wife.

The lassie ran away to fetch it and brought it gladly back.

"Where will I get it again?" she said. "And what shall I call you, goodwife?"

To that the old wife made no reply, but flitted away among the birches faster than you could expect. The lassie wandered up and down the knoll, singing to herself. But at last she grew tired and sat down on the knoll to sleep.

When she wakened the sun had set, and the clear moon was shining down on her. She had lain down with her head resting on the self-bored stone, and as she was just wondering where she would get her lint again, she heard a voice

85

from under her head saying:

> Little kens the wee lassie on the brae-head that
> my name is Habetrot.

The girl put her eye to the bore in the stone and saw right through into the knoll beneath her. It was like a deep cavern, full of spinners, and her friend Habetrot was walking up and down amongst them, watching their work. There was not one whose lips were not long and thick like the old woman's. One was sitting a little apart, reeling the yarn, and she was the ugliest of them all, for she had long thick lips and grey, staring eyes, and a big hooked nose. Habetrot went up to her.

"Make haste now, Scantlie Meg," she said. "That's my wee lassie's yarn, and I must have it ready to give to her as she goes into her mother's door."

The lassie was glad to hear that, for she knew now where she was to wait for the yarn. So she set out for home, and on the doorstep Habetrot was waiting for her. The lassie thanked her gratefully, and asked what she could do for her in return.

"Nothing at all," said the kind fairy. "But don't tell your mother who span the yarn."

It was late now, and the lassie slipped quietly into the house, for her mother was in bed. On the table lay seven black puddings which she had made while her daughter was wandering. The lassie had had nothing to eat all day, and she was hungry. So she blew up the fire again, fried the puddings, and ate them, one after the other, until she had eaten all seven.

Then she went to bed and slept with an easy heart.

Early next morning the goodwife came down. There on the table were seven beautiful smooth skeins of yarn, but there was no trace of the black puddings except a little burning of the frying pan. At the sight the goodwife was nearly out of her head with vexation and delight, and she ran out of the house, exclaiming:

My daughter's spun se'en, se'en, se'en
My daughter's eaten se'en, se'en, se'en,
And all before daylight.

The laird was riding by early to the hunt, and he heard her crying out like a mad thing. "What is it you are saying, good-wife?" he asked.

My daughter's spun se'en, se'en, se'en
My daughter's eaten se'en, se'en, se'en . . .

said the goodwife again. "And if you don't believe me, Laird, come in and see for yourself."

The laird came in and saw the seven smooth skeins, and there was the pretty lass all rosy and fresh from sleep, and he was so taken with her that he asked her to marry him.

She was ready enough and happily consented.

But when the wedding was over, and the bridegroom began to talk of the fine yarn she would spin him, her heart failed her for she could not bear to disappoint him. So she turned it over this way and that in her mind, and at last she went to the self-bored stone, and she called on Habetrot by name to come and advise her.

"Bring your man here at the full moon, my hinnie," said Habetrot, "and I promise he'll never ask you to spin again."

So when the moon was full the lassie brought the laird to the self-bored stone, and leaning their ears to it, they heard Habetrot singing. At the end of the song she got up, and opening a door in the roots of a tree, she called them both in. They went up and down among the rows of spinners, and each one looked uglier than the last.

"They are a strange sight," said the laird at last in a low voice." How is it they have such long lips?"

"With spinning, Laird, with spinning," answered Habetrot. "The bonniest mouth in the world gets badly twisted with pulling out the thread."

"Then we'll have no more spinning for you, my dearie," said the laird. "Do you hear me? You must leave the wheel alone."

"Just as you say, goodman," said the lass, her heart dancing within her.

And from that day the lassie rode up and down the country with her husband, and hunted and played with him, and very happy they were.

All the lint in the place was sent to Habetrot to spin.

Peerifool

There was once a king and a queen in Rousay who had three daughters. The king died, and the queen had to live with her daughters in a small house. They kept a cow and a *kail* yard, but they found that all their cabbage was taken away. The eldest daughter said to the queen, she would take a blanket about her, and would sit and watch what was going away with the kail. So when night came, she went out to watch.

In a short time a very big giant came into the yard, began to cut the kail, and throw it in a big *cubby*. He went on cutting until he had it well filled.

The princess kept asking the giant why he was taking her mother's kail. He answered that if she was not quiet, he would take her too. And as soon as he had filled his cubby he took her by a leg and an arm, and threw her on top of his cubby of kail, and away home he went with her.

When he got home he told the princess what work she would have to do. She had to milk the cow and put her up to the hills, called Bloodfield, and then she had to take wool, and wash and tease it, and comb and card, and spin to make cloth.

So when the giant had gone out, the princess milked the

cow, and put her to the hills. Then she set the pot on the fire, and made a bowl of porridge for herself. As she was supping it, a great many *peerie* yellow-headed folk came running in calling out to give them some porridge too. The princess said:

Little for one, and less for two,
And never a grain have I for you.

But when she came to work the wool, the princess found that she could do none of the work at all.

At night the giant came home, and found she had not done her work. He seized hold of her, and took a strip of skin off her, from head to foot. The he lifted her and threw her on the rafters among the hens.

The same happened to the second daughter. If her sister could do little with the wool, she could do less. So when the giant came home and found her work not done, he seized hold of her, and took a strip of skin off her, from head to foot. Then he lifted her and threw her on the rafters beside her sister. There they lay unable to speak or come down.

The next night the youngest princess said she would take a blanket about her and go to watch what had gone away with her sisters.

Ere long, in came a giant with a big cubby, and began to cut the kail.

"Why are you taking my mother's kail?" asked the youngest princess.

"I'll take you too, if you are not quiet," replied the angry giant.

And indeed, soon enough he took her by a leg and an arm and threw her on the top of his cubby and carried her away.

Next morning the giant gave her the same work he had given to her sisters, and when he had gone out, the girl milked the cow and put her to the high hills. Then she put on the pot and made a bowl of porridge for herself.

When the peerie yellow-headed folk came asking for some, she told them to get something to sup with. Some got *heather cows* and some got broken dishes. Some got one thing, and some another, and they all got some of the princess's porridge.

After they had all gone, a peerie yellow-headed boy came in, and asked her if she had any work to do. He could do any work with wool, he said.

"I have plenty," said the girl. "But I will never be able to pay you for it."

"Never mind," said he, "all I am asking for is that you will tell me my name."

The princess thought that that would be easy enough, and she gave him all the wool.

When it was getting dark an old woman came to the house and asked the girl for lodging. The princess dared not let the old woman come in, and instead she sent her to a high *knowe* in the neighbourhood to lie beneath it for shelter.

It was hot, and so the old woman climbed to the top of the little hill to get some fresh air. There was a crack in the knowe, with light streaming out, and the old woman heard a voice inside saying:

> Tease, teasers, tease;
> Card, carders, card;
> Spin, spinners, spin;
> For Peeriefool is my name.

She looked in, and saw a great many peerie folk working, and a peerie yellow-headed boy running round them.

The old woman thought that her news might well be worth a lodging for the night, and so she went back, and told the princess the whole story.

The princess received the news with great joy, repeating to herself: "Peeriefool, Peeriefool," until at length the yellow-headed boy came in with all the wool made into cloth.

He asked what his name was, and she guessed many names.

But he kept shaking his head and jumping about, saying: "No, no, no!"

At last the princess said smiling:

"Peeriefool is your name."

At that the boy threw down the wool and rushed off in a great fury.

As the giant was coming home, he met a great many peerie yellow-headed folk with their tongues hanging out of their mouths and their eyes bulging. He asked them what was the matter, and they replied that it was from working so hard and pulling out the wool so fine.

That gave the giant a fright, and he said he had a good wife at home, who, if she was safe, never would be allowed to do any work again.

When he came home his wife produced a great many webs ready for him, and the giant was very pleased, and treated her kindly.

Next day when the giant went out, the princess found her sisters. She took them down from the rafters and put the strips of skin back again. Then she put her eldest sister in a big creel and she put all the fine things she could find with her, and grass on the top of it all.

When the giant came home, she asked him to take the creel to her mother with some food for her cow. The giant was so pleased with his princess that he would do anything for her, and he took the creel away.

Next day the girl did the same with her other sister. Then she told the giant that she would have the last of the food she wanted to send to her mother for her cow, ready the next night. She herself, she said, would be taking a walk, and she would leave the creel ready for him.

Actually she got into the creel, and took with her all the good things she could find, then she covered herself with grass.

When the giant came home, he carried the creel to the queen's house. There the woman had prepared a big boiler of boiling water, and when he had set down his creel, they poured the boiling water over him from an upper window.

And that was the end of the wicked giant.

Whuppity Stoorie

Nobody quite knows where Kittlerumpit was, but they say that it lay in the Debatable Land, a tract of land between the Esk and the Sark, two rivers in the south-west of Scotland, long fought over and disputed by England and Scotland.

There on a hillside close to a big fir-wood stood a cottage, and in it lived a woman with her young baby. She was left all alone with her child when one fine day the goodman of Kittlerumpit had gone to the fair, and never come home again.

Nobody knew what had happened to him. Some said he had enlisted in the army of his own free will, while others thought the press-gang had got hold of him, and he might now be sailing in far-away waters.

Anyhow, his wife was left with her small son to bring up, and little else but one sow. People said they were sorry for her, but there wasn't one to lend a helping hand.

But the goodwife of Kittlerumpit was not for giving in easily. The sow was her one consolation. It was due to farrow soon, and the woman hoped for a good litter of piglets. She would fatten them up, and sell them later in the market.

But, one morning, when the woman went to fill the sow's trough with fodder, what did she find, but the sow lying on

her back, grunting and groaning, just about to give up the ghost altogether.

That was a sore sight for the poor woman, and she sat down in the byre, crying her eyes out, more than she had ever done before, even for the loss of her goodman. When at long last she dried her eyes, she happened to look down the brae in front of her cottage, and saw an old woman climbing up slowly. She looked like a well-born lady, dressed in green, with a short white apron, a black velvet hood, over which was perched a steeple-crowned beaver hat. In her hand she carried a long walking-stick, nearly as tall as herself, such as old men and women used to carry long long ago.

The goodwife rose and curtsied to the old woman, saying:

"Madam, I am one of the most unfortunate women alive."

But the old woman wouldn't listen.

"We've all got our troubles," she said. "I know that your goodman's gone away, and that your sow is sick. What will you give me if I cure your sow?"

"Anything your ladyship would like, anything at all," answered the goodwife, never guessing the outcome of it.

"Let's shake hands on that," said the old lady, and marched into the pig sty. There was the sow still groaning while the green woman gazed at the beast for quite a while. Then she began to mutter to herself words which sounded like:

> Pitter, patter
> Holy water.

Taking from her pouch a tiny bottle of something like oil, she rubbed the sow's snout, behind the ears and the tip of the tail with it.

"Get up, beast," then said the green woman, and, no sooner said, the sow rose with a grunt and went to her trough for her breakfast.

The goodwife of Kittlerumpit was overjoyed, and would

have liked to kiss the hem of the green lady's gown for sheer gratitude, but the old woman would have none of it.

"I don't like any fuss," she said.

"Now that I've cured your sick beast, what about the rest of our bargain. You'll not find me greedy or unreasonable; all I want for my good deed, is the baby boy in your arms. And I'll have the bairn," she added.

Suddenly, the goodwife of Kittlerumpit knew who she was dealing with — a fairy woman who wanted her child. She screamed and she begged and she cried, but all to no avail.

"You can save yourself making all that noise," said the old woman, "shouting as if I was stonedeaf." By the law of the fairies, she continued, she could not come for the child till the third day, and could not even take it then if the goodwife by that time could tell her her name.

And with that the green lady departed, while the goodwife fell down in a miserable little heap at the corner of the byre.

When she came to, she cried and cried and cried, and could not sleep a wink all night long. She was no better the next morning, just hugging the baby, and crying her heart out. But on the second day she wandered off into the wood, walking further and further, the child in her arms, until she came to a hollow, an old quarry with a spring at the bottom of it, all overgrown with gorse.

Suddenly the goodwife stopped, listening to what she thought was the hum of a spinning-wheel. And a voice sang:

"Little *kens* our *guid dame at hame*
That Whuppity Stoorie is my name."

"Ah," thought the goodwife. "Now I've got it," and went home a lot easier than she had come out.

She decided to have some fun with the fairy.

When it was time for the green lady to return, the goodwife sat down on the knocking-stone, hiding the baby behind it. Then she put her cap to one side of her head, screwed up her mouth, and howled as hard as she could.

She hadn't long to wait, for soon enough the green dame came up the brae at a good pace. Long before she had reached the top, she called out:

"Goodwife of Kittlerumpit, fine you know what's brought me here; stand and deliver."

At that the goodwife pretended to cry even more, ringing her hands, and falling on her knees in front of the fairy woman.

"O Madam, sweet lady, spare my baby," she sobbed, "and take the old sow instead."

"The devil take the sow for my share," shouted the dame, "I haven't come here for swine's flesh. I'll have the baby, and at once."

"Lady, sweet lady," then shouted the goodwife. "Spare my child and take me instead."

"You must be clean mad," sneered the green lady. "Who would meddle with the likes of thee?"

That was too much for the goodwife of Kittlerumpit, for she thought herself as good as anybody. Holding back her anger, and with a low mock curtsy she replied:

"I might have had the wit to know that the likes of me is not fit to tie the worst shoe-string of the high and mighty princess, Whuppity Stoorie."

At that the fairy leapt high into the air, as if blown by gunpowder. Then she came down with a bump, and ran away and down the brae screaming, as though a bunch of witches were after her.

But the goodwife of Kittlerumpit laughed till she was ready to burst with joy, and bouncing her baby up and down in her arms, she went to the house, singing:

> "A *goo* and a *gitty*, my bonny wee tyke,
> Ye'se *noo* hae your *four-oories;*
> Sin' we've *gien* Nick a *bane* to *pyke*,
> Wi' his wheels and his Whuppity Stoories."

The Wee Folk

Fairies and brownies are quick to punish and to reward, according to people's deserts. They are easily offended, and angry when the rules they live by are broken by humans (although often unknowingly.) Sometimes they covet people's possessions, or even their new-born babes. It may happen that they want their own fairy children nursed by a human mother.

A fine young woman of Nithsdale was sitting rocking her first child, when a pretty lady came into her cottage. She wore a fairy mantle, and carried a beautiful child in her arms, swaddled in green silk.

"Will you feed my bonnie babe for me?" said the pretty lady.

The young woman, aware that the baby was a fairy child, took it kindly into her arms, and laid it to her breast.

"Nurse kind, and never want," then said the fairy, and disappeared.

The young mother kept looking after the two babies, and was astonished to find every morning the richest clothes for both children, and the most delicious food, laid out and ready. The food tasted like bread mixed with honey and wine, and kept fresh until the moment it was eaten.

Early in summer the fairy came to visit her child, and it bounced with joy when it saw her. She was delighted with the child's health and cheerfulness, and taking it into her arms she bade the foster-mother to follow her.

Passing through some scroggy woods, skirting the side of a beautiful green hill, they walked mid-way up. On the sunward slope of the hill a door opened, and they entered the hillside through a fine porch. Then the turf closed behind them.

Once inside, the fairy placed three drops of precious dew on the foster-mother's left eye-lid, after which they arrived in a pleasant land, rich in everything one could ever wish for. It was watered by winding streams, and yellow with corn. The fairest trees enclosed the fields, laden with fruit which dropped honey. The fairy awarded her child's foster-mother with webs of finest cloth and plenty of wonderful food. She gave her boxes of ointments for restoring health and curing wounds and infirmities, promising that her supplies would never come to an end.

As they sat down to rest the fairy dropped some green dew over the woman's right eye, and then bade her look. And to her surprise she could suddenly see a number of people, now dead, whom she had known in life, all doing hard work on the land.

"This," said the fairy, "is a warning. All these people are punished here for their evil deeds on earth. They must work until they have made amends."

Then the fairy passed her hand over the woman's eye, and the magic sight was gone. She then conducted her to the porch where the woman quickly and foolishly picked up the ointment which gave the fairy sight.

For many years to come she enjoyed the gift of being able to see all earth-visiting spirits, until one day she met the fairy again.

She tried to shake hands with her.

"What eye do you see me with?" whispered the fairy.

"With them both," replied the woman.

At that the fairy got very angry, and breathed a hot breath over the woman's eyes, and never again could she see the spirit world, hidden to mortals.

In Corrie Osben lived a shepherd's wife whose child grew very peevish and difficult to nurse.

Neither she nor her husband knew what was the matter with the child or what was to be done with him, until the tailor came to the house to make clothes of a web of home-made cloth, newly come from the walking-mill. On the day after the tailor's arrival the shepherd's wife went to the moors to cut peat, leaving the child under his care till her return.

Shortly after she went away, what did the tailor hear behind him but the sweet music of the bag-pipes. He looked round to see where the music came from, and whom did he see sitting in the bed but a little grey-headed man with a pipe of straw in his mouth, busy playing a tune, to which he sang:

> "Hush! Oranan, Hush! Oranan
> Hush! Oranan, Hush! Ohee!
> Long is the lassie of coming
> To give the Cannan a wee.
> Hush! Oranan . . ."

He kept playing the tune until he heard the woman coming, then the music stopped, and he was again a little child.

The tailor told the woman nothing of what he had seen and heard while she was away, and next day when she went a second time to the moors, he took an egg, emptied the shell of its contents, filled it with water, and put it near the fire. The little old mannie's curiosity was so much excited by what he saw that he turned round and said: "What are you going to do with that, tailor?"

"I am going to heat water to steep malt in," said the tailor.

"Well, I am more than a hundred years old, and never till now did I see an egg shell used to heat water for steeping malt in," said the little man, as he turned away, and began again to play on his straw-pipe. He kept playing the tune of the day before until he heard the woman coming, and then he once more became a little child.

On the third day the tailor told the woman all that had happened, and that in his opinion the child was nothing but a fairy.

"And what am I to do with him?" asked the woman.

"Take him," said the tailor, "to the neighbouring ravine, and throw him over the bank into the water below."

The woman did as she was told, but no sooner had the child touched the water than he became a little grey manikin. He rose to his feet in a great rage, and scrambled up to the steep side of the ravine, threatening the woman with vengeance if he overtook her.

However, she took to her heels as fast as she could and never looked behind her until she arrived at the house. There she found her own child lying at the door, safe and sound, and she was very happy.

In Caerlaveroc in Nithsdale another mother nearly lost her baby to the fairies.

On the second day after its birth and before its baptism her beautiful baby was changed, none knew how, into a weird and hideous elf. It kept the family awake with its nightly yells and would neither be cradled nor nursed.

One day the mother had to go out, and left the elf in the charge of a servant-girl. The poor lass soon sat bemoaning her fate:

"If it wasn't for you, I'd now be out and about, doing my work and enjoying myself," said she.

"Loosen the cradle band," then piped up the elf, "go and talk to the neighbours. I'll soon enough do your work."

The maid did not need telling twice.

Then up started the elf, the wind rose, the corn was chaffed, the beasts fed, and all the chores done as if by magic. After that the lass and her elfin servant rested and amused themselves until the mistress came back. As the elf was restored to the cradle, he again began to yell, and the girl took her mistress aside to tell her what had happened.

"What will we do with the wee devil?" asked the mistress.

"Leave it to me," answered the lass.

At the hour of midnight, and under the servant-girl's instructions, the chimney top was covered, and every inlet barred and closed. The embers were blown up until glowing hot, and after undressing the elf the maid tossed him on the fire. He uttered the wildest and most piercing yells, and in a moment the fairies were heard, lamenting all round the house, and rattling at the window boards, the chimney head and the door.

"In the name of God," cried out the lass, "bring back our bairn."

That very moment the window flew open, the earthly child was laid unharmed on her mother's lap while the elf flew up the chimney with a loud laugh.

Many are the tales of pretty girls and handsome men stolen by the fairies, and this time the water elves and sea fairies, that live in the old haunted hulks in the waters of the Solway, had cast their eyes on the fair wife of Laird Macharg.

Down on the haunted ships they plotted to part husband and wife.

Alexander Macharg, besides being the laird of three acres of moorland, two large kitchen gardens, and the owner of seven good cows, a pair of horses, and six pet sheep, was the husband of one of the handsomest women in seven parishes. Many a lad had sighed for her, and a Nithsdale laird and two Annandale farmers drank themselves to their last shilling through sorrow for her loss.

With the girl married to Macharg, her flesh-and-blood lovers gave up all hope, yet there were certain admirers not easily put off.

The fairies still hankered after the pretty girl.

One day Laird Macharg took his halve-net on his back, and his steel spear in his hand, and down he went to Blahooly Bay, and into the water right between the haunted hulks. There he placed his net, and awaited the coming of the tide. The night was dark and the wind low, and the singing of the rising waters among the shells and pebbles could be heard for several miles. All at once light began to twinkle on board the two haunted ships from every hole and seam, and presently the sound of a hatchet employed in squaring timber echoed far and wide. But if the toil of these unearthly workmen amazed the laird, how much more was his amazement increased when a sharp shrill voice called out:

"Ho, brother! What are you doing now?"

A voice still shriller answered from the other haunted ship:

"I'm making a wife to Sandie Macharg!"

Then a loud quavering laugh running from ship to ship and from bank to bank, told of the joy they expected from their labour.

Now the laird, besides being a devout and God-fearing man, was shrewd and bold. In skill he was certainly more than a match for any dozen land elves. But the water elves are more subtle; besides, their haunts and their dwellings

102

being in the great deep, it is difficult ever to catch up with them if they succeed in carrying their prey to the waves.

The laird rushed home as quickly as his feet would carry him, collected his family around the hearth, and taking his father's bible from the shelf, he proceeded without delay to pray for calamity to be averted.

He first bolted and locked the door, shut up all inlet to the house, threw salt into the fire, and in every way acted like a man skilful in guarding against the plots of fairies and fiends. His wife looked on it all with wonder, but she saw something in her husband's expression that hindered her from asking questions, and a wise woman she was.

About midnight the rush of a horse's feet was heard and the sound of a rider leaping from its back. Then a heavy knock came to the door accompanied by a voice, saying:

"The cummer's drink is hot, and the knave bairn is expected at Laird Laurie's tonight. Mount, goodwife, and come!"

"Preserve me!" said the wife of Sandie Macharg," that's news indeed. Who would have thought it? The laird has been heirless for seventeen years. Now, Sandie, my man, fetch me my shirt and hood."

But the laird put his arm round his wife's neck, and said:

"If all the lairds in Galloway go heirless, over the threshold of this door shall you not stir tonight. Seek not to know why or wherefore — but Lord send thy blessed moonlight."

And the wife did not entreat her husband anymore, saying:

"But let us send a civil message, Sandie, perhaps that I am laid up with sudden sickness? Truly, it's sinful to send a poor messenger away with a lie in his mouth but not a glass of brandy to warm him."

"To this messenger and to those who sent him, no apology is needed," answered the stern laird. "So let him depart."

103

Soon the clatter of a horse's hooves was heard together with the muttered curses of its rider about the churlish treatment he had received.

"Now, Sandie, my lad," then said the wife, "are you not a strange man and a stern one. You put on those hard-hearted looks, and wave your arms as if you were saying: 'I shall not listen to a giddy girl like you.' I am your own true wife, and I must have an explanation."

To all this Sandie Macharg replied: "It is written, 'wives obey your husband,' but we have been stayed in our devotion, so let us pray."

And down he knelt, his wife knelt also with the rest of the household, and all lights were extinguished.

"Now this beats all," muttered the wife to herself. "However, for the moment I shall be obedient."

The voice of her husband in prayer interrupted her thinking aloud, and ardently did he beseech to be preserved from the wiles of the fiends and snares of Satan, from witches, ghosts, goblins, elves, fairies, spunkies and water-kelpies, from the spectre-shallop of Solway, from spirits visible and invisible, from haunted ships and their unearthly tenants, from maritime spirits that plotted against godly men, and fell in love with their wives.

"Nay, but His presence be near us!" said his wife, in a low tone of dismay. "god guide my goodman's wits. I never heard such a prayer from human lips before. But, Sandie, my man, for the Lord's sake, Rise. What light is this? Barn and byre and stable must be in a blaze, and the beasts will be suffocated with the smoke and scorched with the flames."

And indeed, a flood of light, different from a common fire rose to heaven and filled all the court before the house, amply justifying the goodwife's terror. But Sandie remained as immovable as he had been to the imaginary birth of an heir to Laird Laurie. He held his wife, and threatened the weight of his right hand — and it was a heavy one — to all who would venture abroad, or even unbolt the door. The neighing and prancing of horses, and the bellowing of cows added to the horrors of the night. To anyone who only heard the din, it seemed that the whole farmstead was in a blaze, and horses and cattle perishing in the flames. All possible wiles were put into practice to entice or even force the honest farmer and his wife to open the door. But when nothing succeeded, everything was still for a little while, before it all ended with a long, loud and shrill laugh.

In the morning when Laird Macharg went to the door, he found standing against the wall a piece of black ship oak, rudely fashioned into something like human form. Knowledgeable people declared that the piece of wood would have been clothed with seeming flesh and blood, and palmed upon him by elfin cunning for his wife, had he admitted the night visitors.

It was then decided that the woman of timber should be devoured by fire, and that in the open air. A fire was soon made, and into it the elfin sculpture was tossed, from the prongs of two pairs of pitchforks. The blaze that arose was awful to behold, and hissings and burstings, and loud cracklings, and strange noises were heard in the midst of the flames.

When the whole sank into ashes, a drinking cup of precious metal was found, and this cup, fashioned no doubt by elfin skill but rendered harmless by the purification with fire, the sons and daughters of Sandie Macharg, and their children and grandchildren, drink out of to this very day.

Unlucky are those who incur the fairies displeasure.

There was once a man, David Wright, who rented the farm of Craiginnin. His servants, on cutting the grass of the meadow, were accustomed to leaving it to the care of the fairies, who assembled on a hillock nearby, and then came down to do their work among the hay. From morning till evening they toiled. After spreading the hay out before the sun, they put it into coils, then into ricks, and at length took it to the farmyard where they built it into stacks.

The farmer never forgot to repay the kindness of the fairies for, when the sheep-shearing came round, he always gave them a few of the best fleeces of his flock. He flourished wonderfully, but in time he grew old and found his health declining. Seeing that death would soon overtake him, he told his son about the secret of his success, advising him always to be in friendship with "the good neighbours".

Eventually the old man died and was succeeded by his son, who was harsh, grasping and inhospitable. The advice given him by his father was either unattended to or forgotten. Hay-making came round but young Wright, instead of allowing the fairies to perform what they had so long done, and thinking to save a few fleeces, ordered his servants to do the work. Things went on very pleasantly the first day, but on going next morning to resume their labour, the servants were suprised to find the hay scattered in every direction. Morning after morning this was continued, until the hay was of no use any more. In revenge the farmer destroyed all the fairy rings in the neighbourhood, ploughing up the green knolls and committing a thousand other offences.

He soon had reason to repent.

One day the dairy-maid having finished churning, carried the butter to the well to be washed before being sent to the market. No sooner had she thrown it into the well than a small hand was laid upon it, and in a second the bright golden lump disappeared beneath the waters. The servant tried to snatch it, but, alas, it was lost forever. As she left the place a voice called:

> "Your butter's awa
> to feast our band
> in the fairy ha'."

This was only the beginning of trouble.

Not long after horses, cows and sheep sickened and died, and, to crown it all, the farmer himself, returning home on a dark night, got lost in a bog and perished miserably.

After his death the farmhouse fell into decay, and its bare walls are all that remain of it now.

On a farm in Cranshaws in Berwickshire there once lived a brownie. He busied himself working and helping wherever help was needed. At harvest time he cut the corn, thrashed it, and then piled up the straw for the winter. He never asked for any reward but the little bowl of porridge and cream which was put out for him. Master and servants respected the brownie and were grateful for the way he did some of the hardest jobs for them.

Then one year a thoughtless young lad remarked that the straw was not well stacked in the barn. And at once the brownie took offence, and decided that his time at Cranshaws had come to an end, but not before he had taken revenge.

Some two miles away from the farm was a sheer rock, called the Raven Crag, and in the dark of night the furious brownie took all the straw from the barn, and carried it to the cliff. There he shot it over the precipice, shouting all the while:

> "It's no weel mowed! It's no weel mowed!
> Then it's ne'er be mowed by me again;
> I'll scatter it owre the Raven stane,
> And they'll hae some wark e'er it's mowed again!"

On another farm, John Smith, the barnman, learnt that it is wise to heed the fairies' warning.

One day he was sent by his master to cut turf on a green behind a large rock, called Merlin's Craig. After having laboured for a while, he suddenly saw a little woman coming round from the front of the rock. She was about eighteen inches high, clad in a green gown and red stockings, with long yellow hair hanging down to her waist.

"How would you feel," she said to the astonished man, "were I to send my husband to take the roof off your house?" She then commanded him to put every bit of turf back to where he had cut it.

John obeyed with fear and trembling; then rushed back to the farm to tell his master what had happened. But the farmer only laughed, and anxious to cure his barnman of idle superstition, he ordered him to take a cart and fetch home the turf at once.

The man did what he was told although very reluctantly, and nothing happened to him. However, exactly twelve months to the day when the little woman appeared to him, he left his master's work in the evening, with a small can of milk in his hand. But he did not reach home nor was he ever heard of for years. Then on an anniversary of that unlucky day on which he had disappeared, he walked into his house at the usual hour, the milk can still in his hand.

And this is what had happened. Passing Merlin's Craig on that evening many years ago, he suddenly felt ill, and sat down to rest a little. Soon after he fell asleep, awaking again about midnight when, to his astonishment, he saw a troop of male and female fairies dancing round him. They insisted upon his joining them, and gave him the finest girl in the company as a partner. She took him by the hand, and they danced three times round in a fairy ring, after which he became so happy that he did not want to leave his new friends. The dancing went on until he heard his master's cock crow, when the whole troop immediately rushed forward to the front of the craig, hurrying him along with them. A door opened into the hillside, and there John became a prisoner of the fairies.

Then one evening the very same little woman who had first appeared to him when he was cutting the turf, came to him again, saying:

"The grass is green again on our roof; go away home to your own people."

John took to his heels and ran home. And the years he had passed in the fairy hill seemed to him but a day.

Brownies and fairies like food being put out for them regularly, but they hate special treatment.

At the farmhouse of Bodsbeck in Moffatdale a brownie worked hard in and out of doors, so much that Bodsbeck became the most prosperous farm in the district. He took food as he pleased, just simple things, and not even much of them. During a time when the harvest needed hard work, the farmer left an extra meal of bread and milk for the brownie, thinking it but fair to treat him like all his other servants, who got more to eat at harvest time.

But before long he should, alas, find out his error.

The special attention made the brownie furious, and he fled from the farm shouting:

"Ca', brownie, Ca'
A' the luck o' Bodsbeck away to Leithenha'."

And indeed, the fortune of Bodsbeck departed with the brownie, while the neighbouring farm of Leithenhall, whither the brownie had transferred his friendship and his services, prospered.

Another brownie was chased away by a deed, meant kindly, but not at all appreciated by the fairy.

This brownie once haunted the Old Pool on the Nith, a river in the south-west of Scotland, and worked for Maxwell, the Laird of Dalswinton. Of all human creatures he loved best the laird's daughter who had a great friendship for him, and told him all her secrets. When she fell in love, it was the brownie who helped her meet her sweetheart, and in time he invisibly presided over her wedding. When the young woman's first baby was about to be born, it was he who went to fetch the midwife.

Actually the stable boy had been ordered to ride at once and get the old woman, but the Nith was roaring in high spate, and the straightest path, right through the Old Pool, was said to be haunted. So the boy was frightened, and he loitered.

In an instant the brownie flung the mistress's fur cloak over his shoulders, mounted the best horse, and crossed the wild waters. He collected the midwife, but on the way she became uneasy about the road they were taking. Trying to make the brownie stop the horse, she called out: "Dinna ride through the Old Pool tonight. We mecht meet the brownie."

"Hae nae fear, gudewife," answered he. "ye've met a' the brownies ye're like to meet." With that the brownie plunged into the water and carried his companion safely to the other side.

After setting down the midwife at the Hall steps, he went round to the stable where he found the boy still putting on his boots. He took the bridle off the horse, and gave the boy a sound thrashing.

A few days later the minister called at the Hall, and the laird told him all he knew about the faithful brownie. The minister then suggested that not only the new baby but the brownie, too, should be given a Christian baptism. Everybody agreed, and not long after the minister hid in the stable with a dish of holy water, just as the brownie was beginning his night's work. Out rushed the minister, and threw the water over the brownie, loudly reciting the form of baptism.

But he got no chance to complete it.

The brownie gave one yell of terror, and disappeared, never to be seen in Nithsdale again.

On a farm in Peebleshire two dairy-maids were frightened out of their wits by a mischievous brownie.

The two girls were stinted in their food by a mean mistress. One day, from sheer hunger, they picked up a bowl of milk and a bannock, intending to make a secret meal of it.

They sat down on a long wooden form, with a space between them, on which they placed the bowl and the bannock. Then they took bite and sip alternately, each putting down the bowl upon the seat for a moment's space after taking a draught, and the other then taking it up in her hands, and treating herself in the same way.

They had no sooner begun their meal, than the brownie came between them, invisibly, and whenever the bowl was set down upon the seat, he took a draught also. In that way he finished fully as much as both girls put together, and the milk bowl was soon drained.

The surprise of the famished girls at finding it empty was great. They began to question each other very sharply, each suspecting the other of unfair play. The brownie soon let them know what had happened when, with great glee, he shouted: "Ha! Ha! Ha!
Brownie has't a'!"

The two girls got such a fright that never again did they touch food or drink unless it was set before them by their mistress.

The Wee Folk like to keep their kindness to humans a secret, and they punish whosoever tries to intrude.

Once upon a time a boy, called Punchy, suffered badly for his inquisitiveness.

In a small house of a tiny village there lived a little hunchback, a poor, sad creature, deformed from the day of his birth, with weak knees that bent under him and a large lump between his shoulders. He grew uglier and more deformed as he grew up, and there came a time when he hated to leave the house for fear of a crowd of naughty children following him and mocking him. Their cruel ways made him shy, and he often hid in the Willow Brake, a small wood close to his mother's house. Some neighbours got to know about his hiding place, and they nicknamed him the Hunchback of the Willow Brake.

One evening, when the boy had again fled from the teasing children, he met the prettiest little girl he had ever seen, coming slowly down the path. The girl wore a green mantle, held together by a golden girdle, and her green cap was trimmed with silver feathers.

"Where are you going?" asked the girl, who was in truth a fairy.

"I am going to pass the evening in the Willow Brake," answered Hunchback.

"Have you nobody to play with?" then asked the fairy.

"Nobody will play with me as I am not like the other children," sadly replied Hunchback.

She then asked his name, and he told her that it was Hunchback.

"Hunchback!" she exclaimed. "We have been waiting for you. I am called Play of Sunbeam, and I like making people happy. Come with me, and pass the night with my people, and in the morning you will have neither disability nor defect."

And they went away, hand in hand, and walked and walked until they arrived at the Fairy Knoll.

"Shut your eyes, and hold on to me," said the fairy.

Hunchback did as he was told, and presently they entered the grandest mansion he had ever seen. A company of fairies were dancing and singing merrily:

> "Silence, all ye!
> Sunbeam's back hither.
> Hunchback and she
> Have come together."

113

"Success and happiness attend Play of Sunbeam," said a handsome maiden who was more finely dressed than the rest, and who wore on her head a gold crown full of jewels.

"What shall we do for Hunchback?" she then asked. And the little fairy answered:

> "For pain to give him lustiheid
> And, good man's wish, a thriving trade;
> And Play of Sunbeam will be happy."

"Let it be," then said the Queen of Fairies.

Quickly the whole fairy company seized Hunchback, and when he thought that they had pulled him all to pieces, they let go, and, lo and behold, he was as straight as any other boy.

Around him was the sweetest music. Joy filled his heart, and he began to dance with the little people, not stopping until he fell to the ground from sheer exhaustion. He was soon asleep, and as if in a dream he felt the fairies carrying him away through the air, as the soft music became fainter and fainter.

On waking and looking round, Hunchback found himself lying in the Willow Brake. He rose and returned home where he discoverd that he had been away for a year and a day. In that time so great a change had come over him that his own mother scarcely recognised him. But when she heard all about the fairy help her son had received, she rejoiced. He was now as fit and well as any other boy.

Among the youngsters who used to tease Hunchback in the bad old days was one called Punchy. This boy, too, was an ugly little creature, with a big hump between his shoulders. Now, as he saw Hunchback returned as straight as a rush and as gay as a calf-herd, he tried to make friends with him, resting neither day nor night until he had got the tale of the fairy cure. He promised, however, not to tell a living soul, because Hunchback had given the fairies a promise to keep his secret.

Yet the knowledge of Hunchback's miraculous cure proved too much for Punchy, and one evening he went to the Willow Brake, trusting and hoping that he, too, would meet the fairies. But none came. Evening after evening Punchy went, still hoping, and at long last he saw a tiny manikin sitting at the root of a holly bush, gazing at him with a mocking smile.

"Are you Play of Sunbeam?" asked Punchy.

"I am not," said he. "I am Never-mind-who. What is your business with Play of Sunbeam?"

"O, that she will take this hump off me, as she took the hunch off Hunchback," answered Punchy. "Will you take me to the place where she dwells?"

"I will do that," said Never-mind-who, "but it's for you to see how you will get out of it."

"I do not care how I get out of it, as long as I get in, and this ugly hump is taken off me."

The manikin gave a loud laugh, and then went away with Punchy to the Fairy Knoll.

"Who is this come to us without invitation?" cried the Queen, looking sternly at Punchy.

"It is a toad named Punchy whom Hunchback has sent in the hope that his hump will be taken off him," answered Never-mind-who.

"Did Hunchback then break his promise to keep secret what had happened to him?" angrily asked the Queen.

"No, no," replied Punchy, "I wheedled the secret out of him."

"You impudent fellow," shouted the Queen, "you'll get your deserts." And turning to the fairies, she called:

"The hunch on the hump! The hunch on the hump, the hunch on the hump," repeated all the fairies, and then laid hold of Punchy, tossing him up and down until he lost all consciousness.

When he came to, he lay in the Willow Brake, and the

115

hump on his back was twice its former size. Slowly he went home, knowing quite well that this was the fairies' punishment. He carried the big hump to the day of his death but never told anybody about his adventure in the Fairy Knoll.

There are people who can out-wit the fairies without offending them, and to those people the fairies often show courtesy.

There once lived in Rannoch a farmer's son who fell in ill health and who used to go to the hill, morning and evening, to see if the fresh air would help him to get better.

When summer came, and the cattle were driven to the hill pasture, he followed and remained in charge of them until they returned home to the strath in the beginning of harvest.

On a calm, misty day he went away to gather them in the milking fold, but strayed in the mist and was a good long time seeking them before he could see them again. He found them at last grazing in a fine large corrie with green juicy grass up to their eyes.

The day was warm with a drizzling rain falling, and the grass was springing up rapidly from the ground. As the man was tired with the heat and walking on the hill, he sat down on a little hillock to rest a while. He was not long there when he heard a voice coming from the root of every blade of grass at his feet. And the voice said:

"Some of it to me, some of it to me!"

He listened carefully, and again and again the same voice came from the root of every blade of grass in the corrie. He looked to see if he could find out from whom the voice came, but no man, small or tall, was to be seen.

Again the farmer's son listened, and when he heard all the little voices again, he was sure that they came from the fairies, and so he decided to cry as loud as they did:

"And some of it for me also!"

116

Immediately the din of voices ceased, and then he drove the cattle to the fold.

The milk-maids were waiting for them, and wondering what had kept them so long. They began to milk, but before they were finished with half of them, every vessel in the fold was overflowing with milk. They could not understand how the milk had become so abundant in so short a time, and at length they began to praise the weather which, they thought, must be the cause of it all.

The farmer's son listened patiently to all that he heard; but he thought to himself that the milk was not so plentiful on every farm as it was on theirs that day, and that it would not be so plentiful on theirs either had he not beaten the fairies at their own game, and allowed them to draw far too big a share for themselves out in the green corrie.

It sometimes takes cunning and a stout heart to get the better of the fairies.

The mansion of Langton in Berwickshire had a narrow escape from the fairies' wrath which they held against it and nobody knew why.

The Wee Folk had decided to carry the house from the spot where it stood and put it down some miles away on a lonely moor.

On a moonlight night in late autumn the fairies set to work to loosen the foundation of the house, singing gaily:

> "Lift one, lift a'
> Both at back and fore wa' —
> Up and away wi' Langton House
> And set it down in Dogden Moss."

They had just begun to lift the house when one of the family woke up, felt something like an earthquake, and hearing the strange singing, ran to the window. There, to his horror, he saw what the fairies were doing, and he cried out: "Lord, keep me and the house together!"

Hearing the prayer the fairies dispersed instantly, and fled through the air in a gust of wind, leaving Langton House safely in its place.

The miller of Holdean in Berwickshire was drying a grinding of oats brought in by a neighbouring farmer, when, tired after a long day's work, he lay down on some straw in the kiln-barn and soon fell fast asleep.

After a while he was awakened by a peculiar noise, as if the empty space before the kiln were full of people, all speaking together. As he pulled aside the straw from the banks of the kiln, and looked down, he saw a number of feet and legs paddling among the ashes, as if enjoying the warmth.

He listened, and he distinctly heard the words:

"What think ye, o' my feeties?"

And a voice answered:

"An' what think ye o' mine?"

Nothing daunted, though much astonished, the stout-hearted miller took up a large wooden hammer and threw it down, so that the ashes flew about, while he cried out in a loud voice:

"What think ye o' my hammer among
those legs o' yours?"

At that there were yells and cries which turned into wild laughter as a crowd of little people flew up the chimney, and in a mocking tone they sang:

"Mount and flee for Rhymer's tower,
Ha, ha, ha, ha!
The pawky miller has beguiled us,
For seven years to come
And much water wad hae run,
While the miller sleepit."

118

At the head of Loch Ransa in Arran lived a farmer's wife who used to act as a midwife to her neighbours.

On a fine day during the harvest she and another woman happened to be in the field cutting oats. Towards evening a frog leapt with difficulty out of the way of the woman's sickle, and when she saw the poor creature dragging itself out of danger, she said: "There you are, poor creature. You would be better of my help soon."

"Oh! the nasty beast," said the other woman, "if it comes my way, I'll put the point of my sickle through it."

"No! No!" said the farmer's wife, "the poor creature is only crawling about gathering its portion like ourselves."

And the frog was let away with its life.

In a few days a lad, riding on a grey horse, came in haste to the farmer's wife and struck a blow on the door with the whip in his hand. The farmer went out, and the lad said to him that he had come for the wife to attend his mistress, who needed her assistance. The farmer invited the lad into the house to have some food while his wife was making ready for the journey. He thanked the man but said that he was in haste, and that he would wait where he was until the wife was ready. However, she, too, asked the lad to have a morsel of food before leaving. Yet, he remained firm, and reminded the woman of what she had said to the frog while working in the fields. In a flash the farmer's wife knew that she had given herself into the frog's power, and dare not go back on her word now.

She made ready to depart, and the lad promised to see her back safely. The farmer helped his wife into the saddle behind the lad, and off they went, the grey horse at full gallop up the face of the hill. They reached the summit in a very short time, and then the horse turned towards a great chasm which lay between the hill it had climbed and another opposite. When the farmer's wife saw it, she cried to the lad:

119

"Do you expect the horse to leap that great gap?"

But before the words were out of her mouth, the horse went over it like a bird on the wing.

"Well done, grey kitten!" said the lad to the steed that was under him. The words made the farmer's wife wonder, but her wonder was even greater when she looked and saw that the steed which she herself and the lad rode was but a grey cat.

"Now," said the lad to the farmer's wife. "You are going to a Fairy Knoll which is a short distance from here, and there you will attend the Queen of the Fairies. Before we go any further, I shall tell you what you must do when we get there. Be not afraid to take my advice, for I am not a fairy myself, but a human being. I am under spells by the fairies, and have been so for twenty-one years, and I have another year yet to put in before I shall be free to return to my own people again. That you also may have power to return home at the end of your time, take heed what you say and do as long as you are in the Fairy Knoll. Things there will not be as they appear, but do as I tell you, and you will see them as they are, and will no longer be in danger of being deceived by them. Listen then! You will get three kinds of soap, one white, another yellow, and the third red. When you find yourself alone, rub the white soap over your right eye, and it will remove the magic, and then you will see things as they really are. But take good heed that you do not touch your eye, or your brow with either of the other kinds. That is my first advice. Here is the other, and be sure that you do not neglect it. When your time is out, I will come for you, and then the fairies will gather about you and each one of them will offer you something to take with you as a gift. You may take anything they will give you except gold or silver, and I will tell you again what you ought to do with the gifts. But we are now within sight of the Fairy Knoll, and see that you remember all I have said to you."

Soon the door of the Fairy Knoll opened before them, and a mild light was shining through the doorway. The farmer's wife entered, and it was a very grand place indeed. The walls and the ceiling were glittering with gold and silver, and on the floor stood a long table overflowing with plenty of everything, and free to all comers. There was a great company made up of young men and women, clothed in green garments, and surpassing all the farmer's wife had ever seen in beauty. They all welcomed her, and one of them took her into the Queen's chamber.

The Queen rejoiced to see her, remembering her kindness in the reaping field.

And the farmer's wife stayed for a good while with the Queen in the Fairy Knoll. One day when she was alone, she took the white soap and rubbed it over her eye, and lo and behold, everything around her was suddenly changed. The grand palace was turned into a gravel pit, and the tall handsome people into old creatures, small and not beautiful to look at. She never made known what she did or saw, but from that time onwards she felt every minute as long as a day and longed to get home.

At last the lad came and called on her to be ready to leave with him, because the time had arrived when he must fulfil his promise to her husband.

The fairies were not at all pleased at the farmer's wife wanting to go away, yet they gathered round her, everyone offering a gift.

She took all, except gold and silver, as she had been told to do, and off they went on the lad's grey steed. But this time the lad took another road which led them through bushes of briar and thorns. As soon as they reached the first bush, the lad called to her to throw one of the fairies' gifts into the bush. She did so, and that very moment it exploded with a bang as loud as a gun-shot, and turned the bush into flames of fire. At that the woman threw away all her gifts, one after the other, and what had happened to the first, happened to them all.

"Now," said the lad, "had you kept those things until you were home, they would have set your house on fire, and burnt you yourself, and all that is in it. But you have now foiled the fairies' revenge."

They reached the farmer's house in safety, bade farewell to each other, after which the lad rode off at speed.

The fairies have their favourites, and never will they forget the good that has been done to them.

A man from Jedburgh was once on his way to the market in Hawick when suddenly he was alarmed by a frightful noise. He did not know where it came from, except that the sound seemed like that from a great number of female voices. Nothing at all was visible. Amidst howling and wailing were mixed shouts of mirth and jollity, but all he could hear clearly were the following words:

"O there's a bairn born, but there's naething to pit on't."

The reason for all the excitement, it seemed, was the birth of a fairy child, and the fairies were enjoying themselves with great glee, except for two or three of them who were troubled by not having a thing to dress the little thing in.

The astonished man, finding himself amongst a host of invisible beings in a wild moorland place, far from human help, and full of apprehension on hearing the words again and again, stripped off his plaid, and threw it on the ground. It was instantly snatched up by an invisible hand. Then the wailing ceased, but the shouts of mirth were continued even louder than before.

Believing that what he had done had satisfied his invisible friends, he lost no time in making off and proceeded on his way to Harwick, thinking about his strange adventure. At Harwick, he bought a sheep in the market, and returned to Jedburgh. The sheep turned out a remarkably good bargain, and he had no cause to regret his generosity to the fairies. Every day his wealth increased, and he continued till the day of his death a rich and prosperous man.

A woman in Auchencreath in Nithsdale was one day sifting meal, fresh from the mill, when a tiny, cleanly dressed, beautiful woman came to her. She held out a basin of fine workmanship, courteously asking to have it filled with new meal.

The woman did so cheerfully, and within a week the little lady returned with the borrowed meal. She breathed over it, setting it down, basin and all, saying aloud:

"Be never toom."

The Nithsdale woman lived to a good old age, and never did she see the bottom of her meal basin.

Another woman in the ancient burgh of Lochmabon was returning late to her home one evening after gossiping with the neighbours. Suddenly a pretty little boy, dressed in green, came up to her, and said:

"Pour out your dish-water further from your
    doorstep,
It puts out our fire."

The woman realising that she must have emptied her bowls over a fairy dwelling, took care not to harm 'the good neighbours' any more.

She prospered and had plenty of everything she needed for the rest of her days.

And this is what happened to Sandy Crawfurd.

Many a long year ago the country was suffering from a terrible drought. It turned all the green fields and the wooded hills as brown as a withered leaf and as dry as powder. Everything was dried up, and people believed that the day of judgement had come. Some fasted and others prayed, and others again were in great despair. There wasn't a drop of water left in streams and wells.

The drought lasted for two months, and during it many fine cows and sheep died, and small farmers were reduced to a state of poverty. The fairies did all in their power to help the distressed, and it was strange to see their rings and hillocks fresh and green, and never suffering in the least from the great heat.

Now there was a man by the name of Sandy Crawfurd who in his turn had helped the fairies on several occasions, and they can and will repay good deeds as well as anybody, but they will also revenge themselves if they are angered. Sandy was a good man, as good as any that ever lived. He could not bear to see his fellow creatures want, and as long as he had a penny to spare, he was willing to give it to someone in need. His three cows had perished, and they being the principal thing he depended on for support of his wife and family, it was no wonder that he became very downcast.

One night he was sitting by the fire after everybody had gone to bed, wondering, and making a thousand plans as to how he could manage to keep himself, his wife and children alive. Then suddenly a purse fell down the chimney and landed at his feet. He lifted it up and, finding it very heavy, opened it. His astonishment was great when he found it full of golden sovereigns. At the bottom was a small piece of paper with the words:

"Tak' the good goud and buy a koo
you minded us, we've minded you."

Next morning Sandy went away without telling his wife anything. With part of the money he bought two fine cows from a rich farmer, and brought them home. But, alas, in

124

his excitement, he had never thought how he would feed them, and by the time he returned his worries were just as great as before.

But the fairies soon enough settled the matter for Sandy. They told him to drive his cows into the Gowan Dell which at that time was all covered with rushes, gorse and briers. Sandy knew the place well and was about to laugh at the very idea. But afraid of offending those who had been so good to him, he drove his two cows to the Dell.

If he had been surprised at the gold he was given, he was now speechless at what his eyes saw. Every bush and weed had disappeared, and in their stead there had sprung up a beautiful crop of the richest and finest grass. The two cows went to the Dell week after week, and month after month, and still there was no sign of the grass either withering or growing bare. Each cow yielded sixteen to eighteen pints of milk a day, and the butter made from it was better than any other. The fame of it spread far and wide, and people came from all over the place to buy it.

Of course, the neighbours grew jealous of Sandy, and in a short time he had many enemies. Thinking that they, too, might prosper, the neighbours began to drive their own cows into the Dell.

But it was no use!

Not a single cow but Sandy's own gave a drop of milk.

Eventually the drought ended. There was plenty of rain, and the whole country began to recover what it had lost.

Sandy himself got on well, never looking back, and after having made a good pile of money, and leaving his family well provided for, he died, lamented by all that had tasted his goodness.

And the Gowan Dell?

Well, it just looks the very same as it did on the morning when Sandy's two cows first set foot in it.

Some Strange Adventures with Mermaids, Dragons, Sprites, a Witch and a friendly Ghost

Mermaids are wayward creatures, proud, easily offended, and apt to take cruel revenge, as the lady of Knockdolion was to find out to her sorrow.

The old house of Knockdolion stood near the water's edge, close to a large black boulder.

At night a mermaid would rise from the water, and take her seat on the huge stone. There she would sit for hours, singing and combing her long golden hair.

The lady of Knockdolion did not like the mermaid. The mermaid's song, she said, kept her own young child awake. She got angrier and angrier, till at length she ordered the servants to break up the boulder and deprive the mermaid of her seat.

The deed was done, and after nightfall that day the mermaid arrived to find her favourite seat destroyed.

In a fury she called out:

"Ye may think on your cradle — I'll think of my stane,
And there'll ne'er be an heir to Knockdolion again."

Not long after the cradle was found overturned, and the baby suffocated under it.

There never was another baby at Knockdolion House, and the family became extinct.

The young laird of Lorntie in Forfarshire escaped a mermaid's wile just by luck and the presence of mind of his faithful servant.

One evening the laird, attended by a single servant, and two greyhounds, was returning from a hunting expedition.

As they were passing a lonely lake about three miles south of Lorntie, and closely surrounded by dense wood, the laird suddenly heard the shrieks of a female, apparently drowning.

Being a fearless character, he at once spurred his horse forward to the side of the lake, and there was a beautiful maiden struggling in the water, and, as it seemed to him, just about to drown.

"Help, help, Lorntie," she exclaimed. "Help, Lorntie — help, Lor—," and the water appeared to choke the last sounds of her voice as they gurgled in her throat.

The laird, overcome with pity for the maiden, rushed into the lake and was about to grasp her long yellow locks as they lay like hanks of gold upon the water, when he was suddenly seized from behind, and forced out of the lake by his servant. With more foresight than his master, he recognised that the laird was having a trick played on him by a water-sprite.

"Bide, Lorntie, bide a blink," cried the servant, as the laird was trying to push him out of the way. "That wailing madam was nae other, God save us, than the mermaid."

The laird soon enough knew the truth of his faithful servant's warning, for, as he was preparing to mount his horse, the mermaid raising herself half out of the water, exclaimed in a voice of fiendish disappointment and fury:

> "Lorntie, Lorntie,
> Were it na your man,
> I had gart your heart's bluid
> Skirl in my pan."

Long ago there were many terrible fire-spouting dragons, and a great big evil one once lived in a green hollow below the face of a mountain on the west coast of Scotland.

This dragon was the terror of the surrounding countryside. From the lip of the corrie it overlooked the path at the foot of the mountain, to leap down on the unsuspecting traveller, and tear him to pieces. No-one dared attack the monster, nor could any one tell how the dragon could be destroyed.

Then Charles the Skipper came along.

He anchored his boat a good distance out from the land, and between the vessel and the shore he formed a bridge of empty barrels, lashed together with ropes, and bristling with iron spikes. When the bridge was finished the skipper kindled a large fire on board and placed pieces of flesh on the burning embers. As soon as the flavour of the roasting meat reached the corrie, the dragon descended by a succession of leaps to the shore, and then tried to make its way out on the barrels to the boat. But the spikes entered the dragon's body and tore it up badly, so that the dragon reached the far end of the bridge only with great difficulty.

Meantime the skipper moved the boat away from the bridge, until there was a wide space between it and the last barrel. The dragon had not enough strength to leap across, and it died of its wounds at the end of the bridge.

The people who lived in the neighbourhood of the mountain now felt at peace. But, alas, a new danger should soon be threatening them. The old dragon had left one of her young ones behind in the corrie. In time the young dragon grew up, and had a brood of young dragons herself which she kept hidden in a corn stack at the foot of the mountain. There were enough dragons to threaten the whole countryside with their ill deeds.

However, a farmer discovered them, and was brave enough to set fire to the stack. At the sight of her young ones perishing in the burning stack, their mother leapt into the sea below, never to be seen again.

The rock, to this very day, is known as the Dragon Rock.

There was also the Meester Stoorworm, the most fearsome sea-serpent that ever lived, and it took a very brave young man to free the sea and the land of this awesome monster.

The goodman of Leegarth was well-to-do, and farmed his own land. His farm lay in a valley, watered by a burn, and sheltered by surrounding hills. His goodwife was a thrifty and active housewife who had born him seven sons and one daughter. The youngest son was called Assipattle.

Now his brothers looked down on Assipattle with contempt. He ran about all unkempt and in ragged clothes, and he was made to sweep the floor, bring peats to the fire, and any other mean job his elder brothers were too proud to do. They cuffed and kicked Assipattle, and the women laughed at him. Altogether he led a dog's life.

Only one person was kind to him, and that was his sister. For hours she would listen to his long stories about trolls and giants, in which he himself was always the shining hero. These very tales made his brothers even more scornful.

One day the king's messenger came to Leegarth, asking the goodman to send his daughter to live in the palace and be maid to the princess, the king's only daughter. So the girl was dressed in her best clothes, and with his own hands her father made her a pair of rivlins to wear in the palace. Of these she was very proud because in the past she had always gone barefooted.

After the lass had ridden off on a pony, Assipattle's life became even more lonely and dull without his sister there to comfort him.

At that time gloomy tidings came to the people of Leegarth: the Meester Stoorworm, the biggest of all sea-serpents, it was said, was drawing near the land, and this news made the boldest hearts beat faster.

Sure enough, the Stoorworm came and set up its head to the land. It turned its awful mouth landward, and yawned horribly, so that when its jaws came together, they made a noise that shook the earth and the sea. And this it did to show that, if not fed, it would consume the land.

Now there was a mighty sorcerer in the kingdom who was said to know all things. Although the king did not like the sorcerer, believing him to be a deceitful man, he was in the end called to give advice. There seemed no other way to overcome the monster.

The problem was a difficult one, said the sorcerer, but he promised to give counsel by sunrise on the following day.

And indeed, when the sun appeared on the horizon the sorcerer spoke. The only way to satisfy the Stoorworm, he explained, and so to save the land, was to feed the monster once a week with seven maidens. Should this fail, there was only one other remedy left, too horrid even to think of unless the first plan failed.

The sorcerer's advice was taken.

Every Saturday seven damsels were bound and laid on a rock in front of the monster, and it would stretch forth its terrible tongue and sweep the lasses into its horrid mouth.

One day the Leegarth folk went up to the top of a hill where they might see the Stoorworm, and they watched the creature devour its Saturday feast. While all lamented and wondered if there was no other way of saving the land, Assipattle stood up, staring at the Stoorworm.

"I'm not afraid; I would willingly fight the monster," he then said.

At that his eldest brother gave Assipattle a kick and bade him go home to the ash-hole. Yet, on the way home Assipattle persisted in saying that he would kill the Stoorworm. His brothers were so angry about his bragging that they pelted him with stones, and he ran away.

That night the goodwife of Leegarth sent Assipattle to the

barn with a message for his brothers to come to supper. The brothers were thrashing straw for the cattle, and when they saw Assipattle, they threw him on the barn floor, heaped straw on top of him, and would have smothered him had not his father come, and delivered him out of their hands.

At supper when the father scolded his sons for what they had done, Assipattle said calmly:

"You need not have come to my help, Father, for I could have fought them all, and would have beaten every one of them, had I wished to do so."

Then they all laughed, saying:

"Why didn't you try?"

"Because," answered Assipattle, "I wanted to save my strength until I fight the Stoorworm."

At that they all roared with laughter.

"You'll fight the Stoorworm when I make spoons from the horns of the moon," said his father.

All the time there was much grief in the land about the death of so many young maidens, and again the sorcerer was called in by the king, so that he should reveal the second remedy.

He stood in the great hall of the castle, tall and stern, his beard hanging down to his knees, and his hair covering him like a mantle. After a while he spoke:

"With cruel sorrow do I say it, but there is now only one remedy left: the king's daughter, the Princess Gemdelovely, must be given to the Stoorworm. Only then will the monster leave our land."

There was a great silence until the king rose, grim and sorrowful, and said: "She is my only child, my dearest on earth, and she should be my heir. Yet, if her death can save the land, she must die. It beseems her well that the last of the oldest race in the land should die for her people."

The king then asked a respite of three weeks, so that he might offer the hand of his daughter to any champion who would fight the Stoorworm, and this was granted.

Next day the king sent messengers to the neighbouring kingdoms, to tell all men that whosoever would by war or craft remove the Stoorworm from the land, should have Gemdelovely for his wife, and with her the kingdom of which she was heir, and the magic sword Sickersnapper.

Many a prince and great warrior thought this three-fold prize the greatest blessing on earth — a wife, a kingdom, and a sword — but the danger of winning them made the heart of the boldest stand still.

When the goodman of Leegarth brought home the news that the beautiful Gemdelovely was to be given to the monster, there was great lamentation. Assipattle, whatever he thought, said nothing.

At length thirty-six great champions came to the palace, hoping to win the prize. But when they looked on the Stoorworm, twelve of them fell sick and were carried home, twelve were so terrified that they ran home to their own countries, and another twelve stayed at the palace, their hearts sinking.

On the evening of the great day the king gave a splendid supper for the twelve champions who had stayed. However, it was a dreary feast, with little eaten and less said, and though the men drank deep, they had no spirit to make fun. All kept thinking about tomorrow's ordeal.

When all but the king and his Kemperman had gone to bed, the king opened the chest on which he was sitting, and took from it the magic sword Sickersnapper.

"Why take you out Sickersnapper?" asked the Kemperman.

Then the king explained that he had decided to strike the first blow for his own flesh and blood. He ordered his boat to be ready for sail by daybreak.

At the farm of Leegarth that night there were great preparations for all were to go in the morning to witness the death of the fair Gemdelovely. All, that is, except Assipattle who was to stay at home and herd the geese.

132

As he lay in the ashes that evening he could not sleep, and he overheard his father and mother talking in bed.

Said the goodwife:

"You are all going to see the princess eaten tomorrow."

"Indeed, goodwife, and you'll come with us," answered the goodman.

"I do not think I will," said she. "I am not able to go on my own feet, and I do not now care to ride alone."

The goodman then explained that she need not ride alone but would sit behind him on the good horse Teetgong, the fastest horse in all the land.

Still the goodwife hesitated, made excuses, and in the end said she sometimes wondered whether her husband loved her as a husband should love his wife.

"What puts that notion into your head?" asked the goodman astonished. "You know I love you better than any woman on earth. What did I ever do or say to make you think I did not love you?"

"It is not what you say, it's what you will not say, that makes me doubt you. For years I have begged you to tell me how you make Teetgong run so fast, but I might as well ask the stone in the wall. Is that a sign of true love?"

Relieved, the goodman said that it might have been wanting of trust — seeing that women-folk like to gossip — but it was certainly not want of love. Therefore, here and now would he explain the whole secret.

"When I want Teetgong to stand, I give him a clap on the left shoulder; when I want him to ride fairly fast, I give him two claps on the right; and when I want him to run full speed, I blow through the wind-pipe of a goose. And now you know all there is to know."

Assipattle had listened to all this, and he lay as quiet as a mouse till he heard the old folk snoring.

Then he did not rest long. He pulled the wind-pipe of the goose from his father's pocket and slipped to the stable like a thief. There he bridled Teetgong and led him out. The horse pranced and reared madly, knowing that he was not held by his own master. Then Assipattle clasped his hand on Teetgong's left shoulder, and the horse stood like a rock. Assipattle jumped on his back and clasped the right shoulder, and away they went. But when starting the horse gave a loud neigh, and it awoke the goodman. He sprang up, aroused his sons, and all mounted and galloped after Teetgong, crying: "Thief!"

The goodman who was foremost in the pursuit, roared:

"Hie, hie, ho!
Teetgong, wo!"

When Teetgong heard that, he stood still.

Quickly Assipattle got out the wind-pipe, blew it, and the horse went off like the wind.

So the goodman and his sons had to return home, doleful for the loss of Teetgong.

Assipattle arrived at the shore as day began to light in the east. He tethered his horse and walked till he came to a little house where an old woman lay asleep. There he found an old pot into which he placed a live peat from the fire.

With pot and peat he went to the shore again where he saw the king's boat afloat. In it sat the man whose duty it was to watch the boat until the king's arrival.

"A nippy morning," Assipattle called out to him.

"I know that," said the man. "I have sat here all night until the very marrow of my bones is frozen."

"Why don't you come on the shore for a run to warm yourself?" asked Assipattle.

"Because," said the man, "if the Kemperman found me out of the boat, he would half kill me."

"Wise enough," said Assipattle. "But I must kindle a fire to roast a few limpets, for hunger's like to eat a hole in my stomach." And with that he began to scrape a hole in the ground, wherin to make a fire. In a minute he cried out: "My stars! gold! gold! As sure as I am the son of my mother, there's gold in this earth."

When the man in the boat heard this, he jumped on shore and pushed Assipattle roughly aside. And while the man began scraping the earth, Assipattle seized the pot, loosened the boat rope, jumped into the boat, and pushed out to sea.

He hoisted his sail and steered for the head of the Stoorworm. The monster lay before him like a very big and high mountain, and its eyes glowed and flamed like fire. It was a sight which might well have terrified the bravest heart, as the monster lay stretched across half the world, with its fearful tongue hundreds and hundreds of miles long. When angry, the monster could sweep away with its tongue whole towns, trees and hills. The tongue was forked, and the prongs of the fork used as tongs could crush a large ship like an egg-shell or crack the walls of a large castle like a nut.

Assipattle had no fear; he sailed up the side of the Stoorworm's head then, taking down his sail, he lay quietly on his oars. When the sun struck the Stoorworm's eyes, it gave a hideous yawn, one of the many which it always yawned before breakfast. And whenever the monster yawned in this way, a great tide of water rushed into its mouth.

Assipattle rowed very close to the side of the monster's mouth, and at the second yawn the boat was carried into the Stoorworm's mouth by the in-rushing tide.

Through the monster's black throat, on and on, and down and down went Assipattle, till at last the roof of the throat became lower, and the boat's mast stuck its end into it. Her keel stuck on the bottom of the throat. Assipattle jumped out, pot in hand. He waded and ran until he reached the monster's enormous liver. Then he dug a hole in the liver and inserted the hot peat. He blew till he thought his lips would crack, and finally the peat began to flame, and the flame caught the oil in the liver, and soon there was a large fire.

Assipattle ran back to the boat as fast as his feet would carry him. When Stoorworm began to feel the heat of the fire, it spew fiercely, and the floods that arose from its stomach caught the boat, snapped the mast like a pin, and flung boat and man high and dry on land.

The king and his men had withdrawn from the shore to a high hill where they were safe and could watch the agonies of the fearful serpent.

Writhing with pain, the monster flung its tongue high, so high that it struck the end of the moon. Then the tongue fell back to the earth with a terrible crash. It clove the ground, and made a long length of sea where there was once land. That is the sea dividing Denmark from Sweden and Norway. Slowly the Stoorworm coiled into a lump, while the fiery pain made it toss its head. The force of it all knocked out a number of the monster's teeth: some became the Orkney Islands, others the Shetland Islands, and others again the Faroes.

The lump itself became Iceland.

Then the Stoorworm died, but though it is dead, the fire still burns in Iceland's volcanoes.

As Assipattle reached the shore, the king came down to meet him. He took him in his arms, blessed and kissed him, and called him his very own son. Then he took off his own mantle, and put it on Assipattle, and girded him with the magic sword.

A great wedding feast was ordered, and Assipattle and Gemdelovely became king and queen. They lived in joy and splendour, and if not dead, they are yet alive.

If dragons and sea-serpents were fierce, sprites of all kinds lurked in the countryside, and might be malicious or helpful according to their whim.

Shellycoat haunted the sea coast, rivers, streams and lochs.

He was clad in an armour of sea-shells which made a rattling noise when he moved. From it he derived his name. He was ever ready to lure men into danger, mocking them as he did so.

On a very dark night two men were approaching the banks of the Ettrick Water when they heard a doleful voice from the waves, exclaiming:

"Lost! Lost!"

and again:

"Lost! Lost!"

They followed the sound which seemed to be the voice of someone drowning. To their astonishment they found that the voice ascended the stream. So they hurried up the side of the water, and continued their search during a long and wild night. But the further they went, the further away the voice seemed to be. Arriving at the source just before dawn, the voice was now heard from the opposite side of the mountain. At that the weary travellers gave up their hopeless pursuit, and decided to turn and make their way home.

No sooner had they done so, when they heard what sounded like loud bursts of laughter.

"It's Shellycoat," they both shouted at once, knowing they had been tricked by the bogle, but grateful to have escaped his clutches.

Nuckelavee was another horrid monster, never resting from doing evil to mankind. His home was the sea. When he rode on land, he rode a horse as terrible to look at as himself. Some thought that rider and horse were really one, and that this was the shape of the monster.

Nuckelavee's head was like a man's only ten times larger, and his mouth projected like that of a pig and was enormously wide. There was not a hair on the monster's body, for the very good reason that he had no skin.

138

If crops were blighted by sea-gust or mildew, if livestock fell over high rocks that skirt the shores, or if an epidemic raged among men or beasts, Nuckelavee was the cause of it all. His breath was venom, falling like blight on vegetables and as a deadly disease on animal life. He was also blamed for long-continued droughts, because for some unknown reason he had serious objections to fresh water and was never known to visit land during rain.

An old man once encountered Nuckelavee, and had a narrow escape from the monster's clutches.

Tammas — that was the man's name — was out late one night and, though moonless, it was a fine starlit night. Tammas's road lay close by the sea-shore, and as he entered a part of the road that was hemmed in on one side by the sea, and on the other by a deep fresh-water loch, he saw some huge object in his path, moving towards him.

What was he to do?

He was sure it was no earthly thing that was steadily coming towards him. He could not get to either side, and to turn his back to an evil thing, so he had heard, was the most dangerous position of all. So Tammie said to himself: "The Lord be about me, and take care of me, as I am out on no evil intent this night." Then he decided that — come what may — he must face the foe, and so he walked resolutely yet slowly forward. He soon discovered to his horror that the gruesome creature approaching him was no other than the dreaded Nuckelavee. The lower part of the monster was like a huge horse with flappers like fins about his legs, and a mouth as wide as a whale's, from whence came breath like steam from a brewing-kettle. He had but one eye, and that was as red as fire. On him sat, or rather seemed to grow from his back, a large man with no legs, and arms that reached nearly to the ground. His head was as big as a clue of straw ropes, and this huge head kept rolling from one shoulder to the other as if it meant to tumble off. But what to Tammie appeared most horrible of all was that the monster was skinless, a fact which added much to the terrifying appearance of the creature's naked body.

Tammie moved slowly, his hair on end, a cold sensation like a film of ice between his scalp and his skull, and a cold sweat bursting from every pore. But he knew it was useless to flee, and he thought that if he had to die, he would rather see who killed him than die with his back to the foe.

In all his terror Tammie remembered what he had heard of Nuckelavee's dislike of fresh water, and therefore he took that side of the road nearest to the loch. The awful moment came when the lower part of the monster's head got abreast Tammie. The mouth of the monster yawned like a bottomless pit, and Tammie felt his hot breath like fire on his face, and the long arms were stretched out to seize him. Trying to avoid the monster's clutch, he swerved as near as he could to the loch. In doing so, one of his feet went into the loch, splashing up some water on the foreleg of the monster. At that the horse gave a snort like thunder and shied over to the other side of the road. Tammie felt the wind of Nuckelavee's clutches as he narrowly escaped the monster's grip. And away he ran with all his might.

He had sore need to run, for Nuckelavee had turned and was now galloping after him, bellowing with a sound like the roaring of the sea. In front of Tammie was a rivulet through which the surplus water of the loch found its way to the sea, and Tammie knew that if he could cross the running water, he would be safe. So he made a great effort, and just as he reached the near bank he felt the monster's long arms stretching towards him. That very moment Tammie jumped in desperation, and just landed on the other side, leaving his bonnet in the monster's clutches.

Nuckelavee gave a wild unearthly yell of disappointed rage as Tammie, terrified and exhausted, fell full length, but safe into the deep grass by the stream.

To the Laird o' Co, as the proprietor of Colzean in Ayrshire was called, because of the cos or coves in the rock underneath his castle, a tiny sprite proved to be a very good friend.

One morning a small boy, carrying a little wooden can, addressed the laird near the castle gate, begging for some ale for his mother who was sick. The laird told the boy to go along to the butler, and get his can filled. So the boy went away as he was ordered to do.

The butler had a barrel of ale on tap, about half full. Out of it he filled the boy's can, but to his great surprise he emptied the cask, and still the tiny can was not nearly full. He did not want to broach another barrel, yet the little fellow insisted that the laird's order must be fulfilled. So the butler approached his master, and told him of the miraculously large capacity of the small can. He was told to fill the can even if all the ale in the cellar would go. Obedient to the command the butler broached another cask, and had scarcely drawn a drop when the can was full. The little boy then went away, obviously pleased and grateful.

Some years afterwards the laird, being at the wars in Flanders, was taken prisoner, and for some reason or other condemned to die. The night before the day appointed for his execution, he was confined in a deep dungeon strongly barred.

Suddenly the doors flew wide open, and in walked the little boy who had been given the ale. He cried out loudly:

> "Laird o' Co'
> Rise an' go."

This was an order the laird was all too glad to obey.

As soon as he emerged from prison, the small boy took the laird on his shoulders, and, lo and behold, rose into the air. In no time at all he set the laird down at his own gate, on the very spot where they had first met, saying:

"One good turn deserves another,
Take this for being good to my mother."

That done, he vanished, never to be seen again.

It is an uncanny thing to be the guest of a witch, but ghosts can be friendly, and even helpful to people who meet them without fear.

The farmer's wife of Deloraine engaged a tailor with his workmen and apprentices for the day, begging them to come in good time in the morning. They did so, and shared the family breakfast of porridge and milk. During the meal one of the apprentices noticed that the milk-jug was almost empty, at which point the mistress slipped out of the back-door with a basin in her hand to get a fresh supply. The lad's curiosity was aroused, for he had heard that there was no more milk in the house. So he crept after the woman, hid himself behind the door, and saw her turn a pin in the wall. Immediately a stream of pure milk flowed into the basin. The woman then twirled the pin, and the milk stopped. Coming back she presented the tailors with a bowl of milk, and they gladly washed down the rest of the porridge with it.

About noon, while the tailors were busily engaged with the goodman's wardrobe, one of them complained of thirst and wished for another bowl of milk.

"Is that all?" asked the apprentice who had sneaked out after the farmer's wife. "You'll get that all right."

The mistress was out of the way, so he left his work, found his way to the spot he had marked in the morning, and twirled the pin. Quickly the basin was filled. But, alas, he could not stop the stream. Twist the pin as he would, the milk still continued to flow.

He called the other lads and implored them to come and help. But they could only bring such tubs and buckets as they found in the kitchen, and these, too, were soon filled.

When the confusion was at its height, the mistress appeared among them, looking as black as thunder, while she called out in a mocking voice:

"O you lads, you've drained the milk from every cow between the head of Yarrow and the foot of it. Not a single one will give a drop of milk to its master today even though he were starving."

The tailors slunk away abashed and frightened, knowing they had enjoyed the hospitality of a witch, and that only she had the power of twirling the pin to her liking.

The ancient tower of Littledean on Tweedside had long been haunted by the spirit of an old lady, once its mistress. She had been a covetous, grasping woman, and oppressive to the poor. People said that she had amassed a large fortune by thrift and stinginess, and now could not rest in her grave because of it.

In spite of its ghost, Littledean Tower was inhabited by a laird and his family who found no fault with their home, and were not much troubled by thoughts of the supernatural world.

One Saturday evening, however, a servant-girl who was cleaning shoes in the kitchen by herself suddenly saw an elf-light shining on the floor. While she gazed on it, it disappeared, and in its place stood an old woman wrapped in a brown cloak, who muttered about being cold, and asked to warm herself by the fire. The girl invited her to do so, and seeing the visitor's shoes were wet, and her toes peeping out from their tips, blue and cold, she good-naturedly offered to dry and clean the shoes.

The old lady, touched by the girl's kindness, confessed herself to be the apparition that haunted the house. "My gold wouldn't let me rest," she said, "but I'll tell you where it lies. It's under the lowest step of the tower stairs. Take the laird there, and tell him to part it into two shares. One share let him keep, for he is the master here now. The other share he must part again, and give half to you, for you are a kind lassie and a true one. The other half the laird must give to the poor, the old and the fatherless bairns, and them that need it most. Do this, and I shall rest in my grave, where I've not rested yet, and never will I trouble the house anymore till the day of doom."

The girl rubbed her eyes, looked again, and behold, the old woman was gone.

Next morning the young servant took her master to the spot which had been described to her and told him what had taken place. Then the stone was removed, the treasure discovered, and divided the way she had been told.

The laird being blessed with a goodly family of sturdy lads and smiling maidens, found no difficulty in disposing of his share of the money.

The servant-girl, so richly dowered, found a good husband ere the year had passed.

As for the poor, for the first time in their lives they blessed the Lady of Littledean, and never was the old tower troubled again by ghost or apparition.